About Pfeiffer

Pfeiffer serves the professional development and hands-on resource needs of training and human resource practitioners and gives them products to do their jobs better. We deliver proven ideas and solutions from experts in HR development and HR management, and we offer effective and customizable tools to improve workplace performance. From novice to seasoned professional, Pfeiffer is the source you can trust to make yourself and your organization more successful.

Essential Knowledge Pfeiffer produces insightful, practical, and comprehensive materials on topics that matter the most to training and HR professionals. Our Essential Knowledge resources translate the expertise of seasoned professionals into practical, how-to guidance on critical workplace issues and problems. These resources are supported by case studies, worksheets, and job aids and are frequently supplemented with CD-ROMs, websites, and other means of making the content easier to read, understand, and use.

Essential Tools Pfeiffer's Essential Tools resources save time and expense by offering proven, ready-to-use materials—including exercises, activities, games, instruments, and assessments—for use during a training or team-learning event. These resources are frequently offered in looseleaf or CD-ROM format to facilitate copying and customization of the material.

Pfeiffer also recognizes the remarkable power of new technologies in expanding the reach and effectiveness of training. While e-hype has often created whizbang solutions in search of a problem, we are dedicated to bringing convenience and enhancements to proven training solutions. All our e-tools comply with rigorous functionality standards. The most appropriate technology wrapped around essential content yields the perfect solution for today's on-the-go trainers and human resource professionals.

Pfeiffer
www.pfeiffer.com   *Essential resources for training and HR professionals*

About This Book

Why is this topic important?

Appreciative Inquiry for Collaborative Solutions: 21 Strength-Based Workshops is a unique application of Appreciative Inquiry to the world of learning and development. Amid global challenges and complexities, the Appreciative Inquiry worldview asks, "What is it that we do already that is working for us, and how can we leverage our assets and strengths going forward?" The twenty-one workshops in this book are on topics of strategic importance, addressing the desire and need, in our interconnected world, for greater participation and active collaboration in meaning making and resource sharing. Collectively, we have moved beyond data and information collection and knowledge management into new knowledge creation with the imperative to be able to apply new knowledge wisely. These workshops not only deliver positive, new, and wise outcomes, but have the potential to create transformational change at personal, organizational, and societal levels. Appreciative Inquiry as a change methodology is highly impactful in helping us shift how we think, feel, and do business.

What can you achieve with this book?

If you are a leader, facilitator, trainer, or organization development practitioner, here are twenty-one highly engaging, participatory workshops that provide the opportunity for organizations to unleash the creative, the imaginative, and the innovative capacity of their members through their active participation to build organizational capacity. Collaboration, idea generation, social bonding, team building, and learning are natural outcomes of participating in these workshops. Through respectful inquiry, participants become more aware of their own thinking and emotions and learn more about the thinking and emotions of their colleagues as they begin to work together to co-construct outcomes that will benefit all those impacted—individuals, teams, and organizations—and society at large.

How is this book organized?

This book includes an introduction and four parts. The introduction describes the purpose, objectives, content, and structure of the book. Part I provides a context for the Appreciative Inquiry worldview and explains why a positive, strength-based paradigm of doing business and building community is now called for. Part II provides a basic overview of the principles and process that guide the Appreciative Inquiry method, so that you may deliver the workshops with greater awareness, knowledge, and credibility and fully engage your participants. Part III is the heart of the book. It offers twenty-one fully developed workshops that leaders, facilitators, trainers, or consultants can pick up and deliver as they are or customize to their own situations. Part IV provides further tips and techniques for designing your own workshops using Appreciative Inquiry and related strength-based approaches. Electronic copies of all of the handouts and worksheets associated with the workshops may be found at: www.pfeiffer.com/go/appreciativeinquiry

Appreciative Inquiry for Collaborative Solutions

Appreciative Inquiry for Collaborative Solutions

21 Strength-Based Workshops

Robyn Stratton-Berkessel

Pfeiffer
A Wiley Imprint
www.pfeiffer.com

Acquiring Editor:	Holly J. Allen
Editorial Assistant:	Lindsay Morton
Marketing Manager:	Tolu Babalola
Director of Development:	Kathleen Dolan Davies
Developmental Editor:	Susan Rachmeler
Production Editor:	Michael Kay
Editor:	Rebecca Taff
Manufacturing Supervisor:	Becky Morgan

Printed in the United States of America
Printing 10 9 8 7 6 5 4 3 2 1

Contents

About the Website   xiii

Appreciations   xv

INTRODUCTION   **1**

What Is Appreciative Inquiry?   2

What This Book Contains   4

How to Use This Book   7

Value for the Organization   7

PART I   CONTEXT SETTING   **11**

Providing a Personal Context   11

Waking Up   14

Shifting the Paradigm   16

Organizational Contexts   18

Fresh Influences   20

Calling of Our Times   21

**PART II   OVERVIEW OF APPRECIATIVE INQUIRY AND POSITIVE,
STRENGTH-BASED APPROACHES TO HUMAN
AND ORGANIZATION DEVELOPMENT**   **23**

A Symphony of Strengths   23

Appreciative Inquiry   25

Positive Psychology   35

Strength-Based Movement   41

PART III   COLLABORATIVE WORKSHOPS **47**

Introduction   47

Workshop Design Principles   48

Workshop Practice: What You Can Expect   48

Workshop Titles: Affirmative Topics   49

Purpose of the Workshops   50

Objectives of the Workshops   51

Workshop Selection   52

Workshop Duration and Participant Selection   52

Structure of Content   53

Facilitation Process   55

General Guidelines for All Workshops   62

Summary of Process   64

WORKSHOPS

Creating Change Positively   65

Shared Leadership   69

Appreciating Collaborations   73

Valuing Technology   77

Unleashing Creativity for Continuous Innovation   81

High-Performing Teams   85

Compassionate Connections   89

Strength-Based Coaching   93

Respectful Relationships   97

Business As a Positive Agent for Change—Leaving a Legacy   101

Nurturing Diversity   105

Flourishing Communities   109

Peak Performance—Being in Flow   115

Caring for Our Environment   119

Learning at a New Level   123

Working with Integrity   127

Purpose-Driven Selling   133

Global Interconnectivity   139

Generations Working Together   145

Juggling It All!   151

Building Capacity Through Strengths   157

PART IV **DESIGNING YOUR OWN STRENGTH-BASED WORKSHOPS** **163**

Introduction 163

Review of Workshop Design 164

Participants and Leadership 169

Valuing the Appreciative Inquiry Experience 169

Closing Reflections 170

Selected Bibliography **171**

Websites **175**

About the Author **177**

About the Website

Reproducible materials from this book are available online for free.

URL: www.pfeiffer.com/go/appreciativeinquiry

Password: training

 The following materials, indicated by an ''e'' icon in the margins, can be found in electronic format on the website:

Creating Change Positively Worksheet

Shared Leadership Worksheet

Appreciating Collaborations Worksheet

Valuing Technology Worksheet

Unleashing Creativity for Continuous Innovation Worksheet

High-Performing Teams Worksheet

Compassionate Connections Worksheet

Strength-Based Coaching Worksheet

Respectful Relationships Worksheet

Business as a Positive Agent for Change—Leaving a Legacy Worksheet

Nurturing Diversity Worksheet

Flourishing Communities Worksheet

Peak Performance—Being in Flow Worksheet

Caring for Our Environment Worksheet

Learning at a New Level Worksheet

Working with Integrity Worksheet

Purpose-Driven Selling Worksheet

Global Interconnectivity Worksheet

Generations Working Together Worksheet

Juggling It All! Worksheet

Building Capacity Through Strengths Worksheet

Appreciations

I honor and appreciate every single encounter in my life: all connections and relationships have shaped me and show up in my work. I also honor myself for following my intuition and passion, willing to embark on certain paths often not knowing why, how, or where to, but believing that whatever happened would be the only thing that could, and that would be just fine.

Four key people have influenced me profoundly in my profession: Merrelyn Emery, from whom I first learned about true participatory practices and employee empowerment using Search Conference methodology; Harrison Owen from whom I learned to truly trust the people even more than the process using Open Space Technology; John Findlay, whose passion for using technology to help us think and make sense collaboratively provided me the opportunity to write my first, self-published work; and David Cooperrider, creator of Appreciative Inquiry, who continues to inspire me in all that he does, making my heart beat a little faster every time I hear him speak. I acknowledge them all from my heart.

On a personal level, I am abundantly grateful for the support of my colleagues and family. Two colleagues especially, who read my work in progress and helped me in clarifying my thoughts when I was muddled: Cathy Joseph and Dr. Lynda Klau, you know how grateful I am to you both. My husband, Juergen, an extraordinarily gifted man, whose quiet and calming presence and endless support and patience have helped make this my work of joy. I love him dearly.

Appreciative Inquiry for Collaborative Solutions

Introduction

THERE IS A 50/50 chance that you are reading this book because you already know something about Appreciative Inquiry (AI) and/or other strength-based approaches. If you are in the 50 percent who know about Appreciative Inquiry, perhaps you are looking for new AI-framed tools to strengthen your own portfolio and have greater impact on your clients. If you are in the 50 percent who are brand new to this methodology, you are likely to be curious and may be looking for innovative ways to re-engage members of your organization or community to help them reconnect to their original sparkle and personal and professional pride. Strength-based approaches to human and organization development and positive psychology, defined as the study of strengths, excellence, resilience, and optimal functioning in general, focus on members' talents and gifts. Their talents and gifts are their strengths. When people are performing in roles in which they play to their strengths, studies show that performance and satisfaction increase, productivity improves, and they have greater chance at achieving their full potential (Buckingham & Clifton, 2001). This is a radical departure from the long-held view that to help someone perform at his or her best, you work on ovecoming the person's weaknesses. This view is evidenced by the fact that only 20 percent of employees in companies across the globe feel their strengths are in play on a daily basis (Buckingham & Clifton, 2001).

This book was written for change agents, leaders, trainers, facilitators, organization development professionals, and consultants who want to help change the world! It contains twenty-one practical, Appreciative Inquiry framed workshops ready for delivery. The topics of all twenty-one workshops are highly relevant in today's world, and with the Appreciative Inquiry design, they are equally applicable in global corporations, local communities, schools, colleges, universities, government agencies, non-profits, non-governmental agencies, special interest groups, communities of practice, and small business.

My purpose in writing this book is threefold:

1. A facilitator can pick up this book and, with minimum preparation, be able to facilitate any one of its twenty-one workshops. (The optimal facilitator for these workshops is someone with some prior facilitation experience who can follow a process with or without an agenda and who is comfortable with the emergent nature of what unfolds from a group of participants learning together without feeling the need to jump in with answers, be the savior, or be controlling.)

2. All twenty-one workshops are designed to shift the culture in organizations so that they become strength-based.

3. Participation in any workshop will accelerate greater conscious awareness and encourage collaborative mindsets, which can not only improve performance, but potentially transform it.

What Is Appreciative Inquiry?

Appreciative Inquiry is a positive, strength-based, participatory methodology that seeks to discover the best in people and their organizations. To call Appreciative Inquiry a methodology is to use the broadest term with which to categorize it. As a methodology, it is a system of principles, practices, and procedures with strong theoretical underpinnings applied to the field of human and organization development. Appreciative Inquiry is just as much a way of *being in the world* as a way of *doing in the world*—a philosophy and a practice. The foundational belief is that every living system has something that works well already, where people have experienced some success, some satisfaction, something positive in their lives. David Cooperrider, the co-creator of AI as a doctoral student thirty years ago, observed increased employee engagement when there were high levels of "positive cooperation, innovation, and egalitarian governance in the organization" (Watkins & Mohr, 2001, p. 15). Excited by his findings, Cooperrider was encouraged by his supervisor, Suresh Srivastva, to continue to focus on this uplifting research. The name, Appreciative Inquiry, came later, and Cooperrider delights in telling the story. He was sharing the positive and joyful findings of his approach to research with his wife, an artist. In describing how people showed greater positivity and "aliveness" when they spoke of what they valued about themselves and their organizations, it seemed they took on a whole different demeanor and approach when they viewed situations through a valuing lens. His wife, with her artist's perspective, suggested they were seeing the world with an appreciative eye. That was it! This method of inquiry became Appreciative Inquiry.

When you use the Appreciative Inquiry methodology, you open participants to their mental models, belief systems, values, motivations, hopes, and dreams as they share their stories of success. Within this forum, people listen to each other's stories, they share their knowledge, their conversations become generative, and together they produce new knowledge. The opportunity to co-design innovative solutions and ways of organizing is accelerated. Once people begin to shift their perspectives and see themselves and each other from valuing, strength-based perspectives, both positivity and performance are amplified.

The overarching intention of the Appreciative Inquiry approach is to facilitate respectful inquiry into a selected topic to discover what strengths and capacities are already present in the group and the organization at large. With conscious awareness of these already existing foundational strengths—coined the *positive core*—it becomes easier and more inspiring to elevate capacity to embrace change and create organizational value. Once participants have information and knowledge, it is a small step to imagine a future and then go about cooperatively designing ways to get there. For example, imagine you have a team or group of volunteers feeling a little awkward about and resistant to adapting to new technology. You choose to facilitate the workshop "Valuing Technology" from Part III to help shift their mindsets to "We've done this before, and based on the strengths that we already have, we can do it again—even better." In this workshop, the participants inquire into one other's prior and existing experiences with technology. It is highly likely they have had both good and bad experiences with technology. In this workshop, you ask them to focus only on the better experiences, when technology served them or others really well. They discover what worked for them in the past (what they can do already), and from that starting point, they envision how they can adapt to the existing technology, perhaps even enhance it. They also identify the training they might need in order to feel more confident about using it. Participants move from the known to the unknown in conversation with others without an expert having to tell them how. As they cooperatively move toward possibility, resistance becomes a non-issue. This is an example of Appreciative Inquiry being defined as "the cooperative co-evolutionary search for the best in people, their organizations, and the world around them" (Cooperrider, Whitney, & Stavros, 2008, p. 3).

Traditionally, when resistance comes up or issues create tension or conflict so that performance is negatively impacted, or when people are perceived to have a bad attitude, these are seen as problems to be solved and very often they are deemed "training problems." The solution to such issues results typically in organizational members sitting in a classroom with an expert telling them what to do differently in order to change and thereby "fix the problems." Many good tips and techniques can be learned that way, and good outcomes can happen. Alternatively, using experiential learning, we can learn from our own experiences through dialogue and reflection. In relationship with others, as we share our experiences and realities, ideas begin to overlap and co-mingle. Very soon, just as in a high-performing team, we find we are co-constructing new realities and possibilities. Most of us know what else is possible and what we are capable of doing more of. What we need are the conditions and a structure that let us get on with it. We really would prefer to be active participants in our own destiny. Appreciative Inquiry is a way to facilitate such positive shifts in human consciousness and performance.

What This Book Contains

The strength of this book is its application of Appreciative Inquiry methodology in workshop and training design. The majority of the books or articles written about Appreciative Inquiry since the late 1980s have been academic with excellent case study examples. Many, including myself, love to learn this way. This book, however, is different. This book takes Appreciative Inquiry principles and processes and applies them to real, everyday work and relationship issues in a workshop format that allows organizational members to resolve issues and create solutions from a strength-based perspective. For example, you will find workshops on the classic topics, such as team building, leadership, and change, as well as on newer topics, such as cultural diversity, corporate social responsibility, intergenerational mix, and social media, to name a few.

After this Introduction, the book is divided into four parts. Part I provides a context. Without a context there is no meaning. So what is the context that gives meaning to Appreciative Inquiry today? What's happening in the world that strength-based approaches and positive psychology are becoming a preferred way to educate our children, attend to our personal well-being, make a living, and make a positive difference in the world? Appreciative Inquiry uses story telling as a way to help people *bring the best of the past into their current reality and project it into their imagined future*. It is this construct that makes the Appreciative Inquiry experience so powerful and potentially life-altering. The past and present strengths are truly a springboard to the imagined future and offer the grounding that empowers people to embrace the path of destiny. This type of inquiry is in and of itself strengthening. There is much to be valued about our own past stories, if we choose to focus on what we did well, and it becomes clear to us that we can do it again. Furthermore, the rapidly changing global environment with shifting markets, politics, and demographics and the burgeoning of social media tools are just some other contexts that give meaning to the need for increased participation, heightened engagement, users generating their own content, and the will and know-how to create holistic and conscious cultures.

Part II provides a tiny taste of the theoretical underpinnings of Appreciative Inquiry, including positive psychology and other strength-based approaches that are contributing to new models of human and organization development. As I travel the world facilitating Appreciative Inquiry workshops and training professionals in this methodology, I find trainers, facilitators, and consultants become curious about the approach and want to go deeper to learn more about different applications and why and how AI works. In this book, we provide a basic overview of the principles and process that guide the Appreciative Inquiry method so that you can deliver the workshops with greater awareness, knowledge, and credibility, in service of your participants.

Part III, which contains the workshops, is the heart of the book. Each workshop is structured around a series of questions designed from the Appreciative Inquiry perspective to move participants forward in a positive way. Each workshop agenda is framed from the perspective of "What is it that we do already that is working for us, and how can we leverage our strengths going forward?" Participants develop an expanded understanding of issues pertaining to a specific topic and generate ideas, proposals, and actions for implementation. The design of the workshops, by following the Appreciative Inquiry structure and process, differs dramatically from the traditional problem-centered approach so prevalent in our organizations, institutions, and families. The affirming language and questioning sequence move participants quickly to a state of flow and full engagement. When we are in a flow state, we feel so focused on an activity that we are fully energized, with high levels of concentration and fulfillment.

As result of the Appreciative Inquiry process, participants:

- Discover the already-existing strengths of individuals and the organization—we name these strengths and assets the "Positive Core"
- Shine the light on the best of what already exists so the collective brilliance is refracted into the organization's imagined future
- Co-construct what can be done (practically) and should be done (morally) in building future capacity
- Expand and amplify that which works and stay open to continuous renewal, learning, and innovation

To achieve such outcomes in a short time frame may surprise. With experienced, well-directed facilitation and the structure and affirmative language of the question sets, participants stay highly engaged and focused. Existing knowledge is shared and new knowledge is co-created. At the conclusion of most workshops, the facilitator invites participants to say what they valued about the experience and share their personal commitments. In these seemingly small acts lies the possibility of new, potentially grand beginnings.

All workshops have a framework to help leaders and team members energize their organization and engage others in collaborating for meaningful, sustainable solutions. The strength-based design enables a proactive, positive approach, emphasizing human and organizational strengths to problem solve, rather than putting the greater percentage of energy and investment into perpetuating the downward spiral of negativity by focusing only on the "problem side" of problems. The design, from the outset, invites participants to pay full attention to one another, as they tune into each other's stories of excellence. Those who, until this point, perceive they do not possess "good listening skills" or empathy will discover they can actually perform these virtuous skills. Turning to another and being there fully for another, and to experience another being fully present for you, produces a positive affect that expands and amplifies flourishing outcomes.

In a very short time, less than half a day, the tone and content of the workshop will have opened up the participants to reconnect with their personal strengths, discover their collective strengths and capabilities to imagine what else is possible, and co-design what is required to produce the results that will make a sustainable difference locally and in the world.

Part IV provides more practical guidance with tips, techniques, and insights so facilitators can expand their repertoires and design their own workshops and training agendas following the Appreciative Inquiry principles and process. It is easy to tweak the twenty-one workshops in this book, if desired, to make them as highly relevant as you need, adapting them, overlaying any language or issues important to your group. As facilitator or leader, you can customize the workshops to suit specific business issues and organizational challenges or school or community contexts. The tips in Part IV will keep your modifications aligned with the Appreciative Inquiry framework.

A purpose of this book is to make it easy to facilitate from a strength-based perspective and to provide some tools to be able to design workshops and trainings following the Appreciative Inquiry etiquette. The goal of any Appreciative Inquiry intervention—large or small—is for the community to own its own destiny and keep the iterative cycle alive for continuous learning and adaptation. It is desirable, therefore, that after facilitating one of the workshops in this book, there are follow-up meetings to continue to expand on the momentum, honoring contributions and changes. It is important to keep the tone the same as the original workshop to maintain continuity as you transition to the new ways participants have collectively and collaboratively begun to co-create.

How to Use This Book

If you are trained in Appreciative Inquiry, from Case Western Reserve University, Taos Institute, NTL Institute, or from any of the practitioners accredited by these or other reputable global institutions teaching Appreciative Inquiry, you are likely to be very curious and turn directly to Part III to decide which workshops will address your first need. If you have been a participant in an AI summit, or attended an introductory session on AI, or have read something about it, you are strongly advised to read Parts I and II, especially Part II, and invest in Appreciative Inquiry books and peruse websites recommended in the resource section to learn more. If something is unclear to you, look for your answer in Part II or Part IV. Both provide step-by-step procedures for different elements of the process. If context and knowing a little more about the author interests you, then Part I will address your curiosity.

Value for the Organization

In a business setting, selecting a workshop will be contingent on the workshop whose topic and content will advance the business strategies, support leadership, and engage and empower employees to build their own and their organization's capacity. Fortunately, the appreciative design of these workshops will deliver outcomes that will positively impact the people and business performance, especially if you have the mental model and an organizational culture that embrace a strategy that good business and good relationships are intrinsically interwoven.

The biggest question you can be conscious of as you facilitate a workshop is "How do I create value not only for those physically present, but for the wider stake-holding community beyond the workshop, whose presence is also felt." They could be customers, suppliers, leaders, team members, shareholders, and families. In the context of these workshops, the question of creating value bridges the so-called intangible benefits of heightened employee engagement, productive teamwork, enlivened creativity, enhanced reputation, knowledge sharing, trust, and loyalty, as well as the more traditionally measured benefits of increased productivity, sales, revenues, profitability and reduced costs, turnover, complaints, grievances, and waste.

What you are looking for is a correlation between positive human performance and positive financial results. If you can track positive performance such as satisfied customers, healthier and more highly motivated staff, and other relevant indicators of improved performance and then correlate them with improved financial results, you are building the business case that so-called "soft" positive interventions produce real "hard" positive results. The notion of well-being then becomes a contender for measurement. If the culture of the organization is already predisposed to viewing the world through a valuing lens and sees the dynamic relatedness across the whole system, then the chance of creating and amplifying a flourishing community is heightened.

"The executive vocation in a post-bureaucratic society is to nourish the appreciative soil from which affirmative projections grow, branch off, evolve, and become collective projections. Creating the conditions for organization-wide appreciation is the single most important message that can be taken to ensure the conscious evolution of a valued and positive future."
—DAVID L. COOPERRIDER, *Positive Image, Positive Action: The Affirmative Basis of Organizing*

Part I

Context Setting

PART I PROVIDES a context for this book. The last ten years have been boom years for the strengths movement and positive psychology. Appreciative Inquiry has been delivering *positive revolutions in change* to all sorts of contexts for thirty years. These new positive, strength-based methods for human and organization development have arrived, and we are ready.

Providing a Personal Context

"Curiosity killed the cat" was one of the many proverbs my grandmother delighted in repeating to me, as a very young child, every time I poked my head into something new or asked "Why?" It silenced me, as I was upset by the idea of "killing cats." My mother, too, after endless "Why?" questions, in frustration would sigh, "Because I said so" or "'Y' is a crooked letter that can't be made straight." I had to pause to think hard about trying to straighten the letter "Y" and wouldn't dare ask, "Why does it need to be straightened?" Even my father would tell me, "Mind your p's and q's." I couldn't fathom that one. In spite of these early reprimands, it seems my curiosity, love of learning, and desire to seek out new ideas have been my constant guides. These days, whenever I am in a new territory, I am called to go further to explore what's around the corner, over the hill, or beyond the horizon. I am truly satisfied when I discover for myself what I can learn and what new ideas come up that stimulate possibility-thinking and what-if scenarios. After years of following these instincts, I know now that curiosity, love of learning, collecting ideas, and seeing the big picture are my best attributes, or my signature strengths. I am most satisfied when I am playing or working to these strengths.

Little surprise, then, that when I first heard the term Appreciative Inquiry, my neurons lit up and sparks were firing, especially as a trusted colleague had tantalized me with, "You will love this—it's all about finding what works best in people and organizations; it's been called a positive revolution in change." As a facilitator of change, my strength is designing and facilitating workshops from a smorgasbord of tools and methodologies I have learned over the years, and I am constantly on the lookout for new, relevant tools to add to my toolkit. Finding Appreciative Inquiry, or Appreciative Inquiry finding me, was a gift. It has deepened, broadened, and enhanced my way of living and working. Here is a practical framework that looks at the world with a valuing lens. It addresses problems from the perspective of what's working, instead of what's broken, looking for the best in people and situations, not the worst. The worldview of Appreciative Inquiry, seeing people and their organizations as sources of strength and vitality, is a paradigm shift because it begins with the positive and therefore approaches change from that perspective. Instantly, Appreciative Inquiry resonated powerfully. It connected with my instinctive approach to see the glass half-full instead of half-empty. People and organizations are living systems not only amassed with problems waiting to be solved but also filled with unlimited capacity for human relatedness, innovation, creativity, and excellence waiting to be appreciated.

As a life-centric change process, Appreciative Inquiry pays attention to the best in us, not the worst; to our strengths, not our weaknesses; to possibility thinking, not problem thinking. Appreciative Inquiry is an affirming way to embrace organizational change. It is a change method with the perspective that every system, human and otherwise, has something that works right—things that contribute to its aliveness, effectiveness, and success, connecting it in healthy ways to its stakeholders and the wider community. When we are open with each other to truly connect, we find our intersect points, and from that shared place of common humanity we begin to share dreams and aspirations, addressing problems in different ways. One of the ways we do this is story telling. It is through telling our stories that we transcend our differences as we discover our universal connection with others. "Remember, you don't fear people whose stories you know. Real listening always brings people closer together" (Wheatley, 2002, p. 145). With that mind, I begin with some of my stories.

At the tender age of sixteen, my stated career goal was to "maximize people's potential." I didn't know what it truly meant at the time, other than I wanted to help people live their best lives. I followed that intuition, and many years later, I would even say it is my calling. My "maximizing people's potential" has taken on multiple guises. I have contributed in many ways, in a wide variety of roles, switching careers across industries, countries, and cultures, always keen to embrace the newest technologies and evolving methodologies. Over time, continuing to learn and grow, I live with increased conscious awareness. This means two things: first, that I pay attention to as many of the thoughts, feelings, images, connections, judgments, impulses, and desires that flash in and out of my wakeful state and reflect on their appropriateness for the context; and second, that I pay increasing attention to the mystery and magnificence of life itself, cultivating a wonderment, gratitude, and desire to contribute positively to evolving our human spirit such that it benefits all beings and our entire universe.

It was in 2003 that I signed up to experience and learn about Appreciative Inquiry from its co-creator, David Cooperrider, at Case Western Reserve University. Approaching change from the mindset of existing strengths and discovering the healthiest, most alive experiences sounded most compelling. Here was a way to embrace wholeness: to view organizations as centers of human relatedness, where members are invited to discover their strengths through learning about and with one another, sharing their high-point stories of performing at their best. Here was a way to build on these stories of excellence by using our imaginative capacities to dream what we aspire to and, furthermore, to co-design flourishing environments for work and/or play that are a fusion of our own grounded realities and our highest aspirations. It was also thrilling to learn how positive psychology builds our resiliency and contributes to health and happiness over time. I was re-energized to find a method that initiated change from a healthy, positive foundation instead of the traditional "It's not working"/"We've got a problem" mindset. Reflecting on my personal and professional life, I became aware that, had I been more conscious of my innate talents and strengths *earlier* in my life, how much more joyful, productive, efficient, and healthy that might have been … and, that's speaking just for me. Imagine the flow-on effects to all those I have lived and worked with. Their lives would have been so much easier as well! While I intuited my career goal to maximize people's potential very early in my life, it is taking a lifetime to increase my knowledge, find congruent tools, and develop my skills to the point at which they have become interwoven into who I am.

Waking Up

This book is written for facilitators, change agents, trainers, and leaders. It's a practical how-to book to help bring Appreciative Inquiry and its positive, strength-based approaches into organizations and communities easily, effectively, and efficiently. As you continue to read this book and learn more about these approaches, you will become aware very quickly, if you haven't already, that Appreciative Inquiry is more than a practical method to be able to do things in an energized, collaborative, and generative way; it is very much a way of being in the world, a philosophy. As the creator of the collaborative workshops, my intention in writing this book is to inspire you to experience the value and joy that comes from working and living with increased awareness of your strengths, building your positivity ratio (Fredrickson, 2009), and become more consciously aware of all your thoughts, feeling, actions, and interactions in all ways at all times. Appreciative Inquiry is a process that integrates all three of these goals. It is a pathway to building trusting, flourishing, conscious environments.

As trainers, we generally encourage our participants to work toward unconscious competence in acquiring new knowledge, skills, and attitudes. The intention is to be able to perform at a level of competence without conscious awareness: that is, we can do it without thinking. As our skill level increases, our performance becomes easier. Remember how it was to learn a new computer program? Before we launched into such a new endeavor, we had no level of competence: we didn't know what we didn't know. We describe this initial stage as *unconscious incompetence*. We muddled through, acknowledging soon enough that we were not fully competent. We realized we needed some training or coaching to attain a level of competence.

With training and coaching, we worked at it and we improved. We performed some functions from memory, but for others we had to refer to the manual, and still we would make a number of errors. We felt a little awkward and self-conscious; we were not yet fully confident. However, we had come to a good place. We had become aware of what we didn't know, so we moved to a level of *conscious incompetence*. With increased awareness of our incompetence, we took more lessons and focused on what we needed to learn. Our performance improved even further and our initial stress levels lessened as we became more conscious of our growing competence. Performing now with greater ease and comfort, we had attained a level of *conscious competence*. With even more practice and investment of our time, we reached a level of performance wherein we could use the software program without referring to manuals or having to consciously access steps from memory. It became "second nature to us"—just like riding a bike. We could just do it. We were operating at a level of *unconscious competence*. We had moved from *unconscious incompetence* to *conscious incompetence* to *conscious competence* and then *unconscious competence*.

While performing at a level of unconscious competence works for us at both neurological and physical levels to protect us from stimulus overload and help us to do things efficiently, it is not enough. It seems we are awakening from the complacency that comes from operating on autopilot and performing in a perfunctory way. Staying at this level will not maximize our full potential. Since the beginning of this century, neuroscience has taught us so much about the magnificence of the human brain, which is extremely exciting, as we think about all there is still to learn. It is not only in science that exciting discoveries are being made, but technologically and sociologically we are also making speedy progress. As next-generation trainers and developers, our work is much more than training to develop skills, knowledge, and attitudes so that our clients perform at a standard of unconscious competence. Today, there is an imperative to move beyond unconscious competence. To participate fully in the complex and interdependent world of which we have always been a part, it behooves us to embrace our lives as fully conscious human beings: to be awake to our whole selves and step up to our highest potentials so we can live our lives to the fullest. To be the best we can be is to maximize our potential, to recognize and honor our strengths, to continue to develop them and facilitate others to invest in their own strengths.

To help us move in such a direction, we need to develop another competence: a *reflective competence*. The term, used originally in the fields of education and social work, refers to the ability to be fully aware of oneself, one's thoughts and feelings in a given situation—namely, seeing the dynamics as they are being played out in the full context of the situation. It could be equated with taking a "third position" where you are the fly on the wall observing all that is going on, including how you are simultaneously constructing your part in the situation and responding to it and those involved. At the same time, you are in the movie and watching the movie run before your very own eyes. In the organizational context, we have moved beyond simple data collectors, information users, and knowledge managers to co-creators of new knowledge. The hope and possibility of our time is to apply our new knowledge, skills, and increased consciousness in our homes, schools, hospitals, communities, businesses, and corporations with wisdom.

Shifting the Paradigm

> The historian of science may be tempted to exclaim that when paradigms change, the world itself changes with them.
>
> —Thomas Kuhn

As a student at Sydney University, in Sydney, Australia, I was informed that it took about thirty years for new theories about our world to make it into the mainstream. Making it into the mainstream means that new theoretical concepts and knowledge become accepted, integrated, or even supersede the prevailing paradigms. Despite our electronic evolution in the last twenty years and the speed and volume at which information can be shared, still we have been slow to act on new knowledge and apply it wisely. Our human capacity to hang on to what is familiar and comfortable is hardwired. "Why fix it, if it ain't broke?" has been a dominant worldview that supports a prevailing paradigm that the only time to improve a system—human or otherwise—is to wait until something fails, goes wrong, or is a weakness or a problem.

This old paradigm of focus first on weakness is played out every day in most of our homes, our schools, our institutions, and our places of work and worship. The behaviors, the processes, the decisions that are described as weaknesses or problems are the first to grab our attention. We focus on the things that "need fixing." As a consequence, those behaviors, thoughts, feelings, decisions, and processes that are working well and bring us successes don't attract the same attention or the investment of resources. We invest energy, money, time, intellect, and emotion into things that don't work for us instead of putting energies into those things that will give us an easier and a much-amplified return for our efforts and investments. Simply, what we focus on gets done. Punters at the racetrack do not place their hard-earned money on the weakest horse in the race. They bet on the best and the strongest. Owners and trainers of racehorses invest in nurturing and developing the strengths of each individual horse. It's not to say that they discount or ignore their weak areas. They work on the principle that the return on investment will come from developing what is already a natural strength in each horse.

When training for triathlons, cycling was my strength, running was in the middle, and swimming was my weakest stage. To perform at my best, it was the cycling I needed to excel at. I could get into the zone when I cycled. I was at one with the bike, torso parallel to the road, legs dancing on the pedals, feeling the exhilaration of my rhythmic cadence, the wind flowing over me as I challenged myself to go faster and faster. It was hard work and it was pure joy. I trained in running, but it took much more effort to feel pleasure above pain. No matter how much I trained, I would never bring my running up to a standard that would exceed my performance on the bike. When it came to swimming, I trained just to be able to compete—damage control, as it's known. Swimming was hard work for me. I lacked the same joy I experienced in cycling. Had I invested all my time in my weakest stage, I would have jeopardized my overall performance and would have certainly dampened the pleasure and rewards I got out of participating in triathlons.

Similarly, if you were the coach of a successful swimming team, you'd know the strengths and weaknesses of all your team members. In order to get the best out of the team, you'd invest greater effort on developing the strengths of each team member to optimize his or her performance. You would also work with team members to overcome their weaknesses for necessary damage control. The biggest investment of your time, effort, and money, however, would be in building the strengths of each team member. You would not do it the other way round—focus on individuals' weaknesses at the cost of their natural talents and strengths.

It seems we know this in the sports arena. Yet, when it comes to organizational contexts, don't we do it the other way round? A vast majority of leaders still think we need to eliminate weaknesses in order to obtain optimal performance. Peter Drucker, one of the most influential thinkers on leadership and management, stressed that the role of leadership is to build on organizational strengths so that weaknesses seem irrelevant. Weaknesses cannot be ignored. But to develop and improve performance, it is more resourceful to focus on what already works well. At one time, I was contracted to coach a number of highly talented women in a professional services firm. All six clients came to their first coaching session with their 360-degree performance review reports. The first gesture of each person was to go the end of the document and point to the feedback of her manager with the comment, "These are my weaknesses. These are the areas my manager wants me to work on." Each woman paraphrased her manager's desire for her to address her weaknesses. Each considered the manager's perspective to be fair and agreed focusing on these areas would help her advance in her career with the firm.

I listened respectfully before I spoke: "It is important to have this information. It's only one part of the story, not the whole, and we'll get there. For now, what do you think you do best in your role, when you are working to your best, and you feel most productive; when the work may be challenging, and at the same time most satisfying; when you feel fully engaged and time just seems to fly?" 99.9 percent of the time when I set the scene in this way, the response is silence, a puzzled look, a defocused glaze to access memory and then a pronounced physiological shift happens. Sheepish smiles light up their faces, a softening of the shoulders precedes a more relaxed posture, and then they struggle to respond. It usually is a struggle at first, because our education system traditionally seeks to correct what's bad and not reward what's good. Most of us have difficulty talking about our strengths and talents up-front. In support of the strengths movement, there is new research in the field of neuroscience that shows brain cells learn from our successes rather than our failures. The corollary is that we are more likely to be successful when we deploy our strengths with confidence rather than struggle with overcoming our weaknesses with difficulty.

Organizational Contexts

Organizational cultures vary, just as human personalities vary. Many organizations are embracing new methods and tools that bring all voices to the table. Participatory, inclusive decision making and increased global collaboration with the help of social media platforms to level the playing field are becoming more common, facilitating our capacity to be more experimental, playful, and engaged. Still, in most organizations, the starting point is to focus on what is broken and then call for change or a training program only when leaders or managers perceive employees are not performing. "It's a training problem," they complain. How many of us have been brought in to fix many "training problems" after a major change implementation failed to include informing (let alone including) the employees of new strategies, organizational restructure, new technologies, systems, processes, policies, or procedures. The expectation was that employees would slot into whatever the new design was and keep the organization running smoothly without support or strategies for transitioning to the new. Psychologically, one of the ways of coping with the feelings of anxiety and frustration is to defend against them by regressing to learned helplessness, and with that come dependent behaviors and downtrodden, discouraged thoughts and feelings.

Years ago, I led a team of twelve training consultants for a major global professional service firm in Melbourne, Australia. My boss called me in one day, a little frustrated that I wasn't managing my team as tightly as he wanted me to. He handed me the marker pen, pointed to the huge whiteboard that hung on the wall in his huge corner office, and asked me to draw my organizational chart and reporting structure. Somewhat surprised at his request, yet without hesitation, I drew a circle and placed myself between the center and the edge of the circle and consciously placed the various team members within the circle, as I perceived them to be in relation to each other and to me. I placed my boss at the circle's edge.

I had believed him to be a temperate man. (He was an ex-minister.) As I drew my organizational chart, I felt him bristling to my side. He went red in the face and spoke to me with a tense jaw in a very restrained tone, "No wonder you're having trouble managing!" He took the marker pen from my hand and aggressively drew a traditional organizational tree structure on the whiteboard. He was at the top of the tree (in a box) with a vertical line to me (in a box) beneath him and then beneath me, vertical lines to all the twelve consultants (they were not in boxes). I attempted to explain the thinking or philosophy behind my chart, but I wasn't heard. That experience helped me realize my natural talents and strengths, after five years of service, could be better utilized elsewhere. I came to the conclusion that I had the potential to flourish in a different environment.

The command-and-control organizational structure is not an optimal one to facilitate human flourishing. Much has been written about the dampening effect of the command-and-control structure on willingness to assume responsibility, exercise creativity, and show innovation. Over time, command-and-control structure creates cultures of dependency. When the boss makes all the decisions and takes all the credit, employees' will to assert any form of leadership is diminished. In such contexts, employees do the best they can with resources available, willing to assume full responsibility for their actions, being accountable to their bosses, but often it all stops there. Their sense of pride in work well done is passed over without receiving fuller and broader acknowledgment or having the opportunity to earn wider visibility. Over time, this type of unsupportive climate wears thin; motivation and morale begin to spiral downward. A discouraged, disempowered workforce, whose ideas are not listened to and whose full potential is not realized, does not perform optimally. The spirit of ownership, vitality, engagement, and possibility-thinking diminishes.

Fresh Influences

From the perspective of systems dynamics, other forces in the open system—economy, politics, environment, science, society, and culture—are finally being acknowledged for their influence at the local level—our places of work, our communities, and regions. We are more aware than ever before of the interdependency of all these dynamics. The interplay of these elements seems to have sped up, meaning the time to market has also sped up, requiring decisions to be made down the line by those performing the tasks. Waiting for executives to own and endorse all the decisions no longer produces the best results. Moreover, the shifting demographics of the workforce with the influx of Generation Y, the Millennials, or the Net Gen (all names for the same generation born between 1977 and 1999), who are beginning to enter our workforce and who will constitute the dominant employed demographic within ten to fifteen years, is bringing a whole new complexion to the workplace. This generation has new and refreshingly different sets of expectations. It has been labeled the "can-do" generation. Members of this generation had parents who were able to respond generously to many of their needs, which is perhaps why they are also described as the pampered generation. They are the most technologically connected, savvy, and socially networked generation. They are virtual problem solvers, seeking opportunities to contribute in friendly, flexible environments. This new workforce is goal-oriented, with a positive attitude, and is open to a sharing, collaborative team culture in which everyone is treated respectfully. They possess a strong confidence, they embrace challenge, they want development, and they thrive on recognition and feedback. They seek work that is meaningful and expect leaders to be participative and to demonstrate respect for their knowledge and skills, creativity and entrepreneurial spirit.

Could it be, looking through the lens of Maslow's (1943) Hierarchy of Needs, that members of Net Gen, in the affluent parts of the world at least, having their physiological, safety, and belonging needs met early, enter the workplace ready to fulfill their esteem and achievement needs much sooner than the generations before them? In fact, their need for self-actualization seems to be their modus operandi—they want to change the world. When shelter, food, safety, and comfort are taken for granted, and feeling loved and cared for promotes self-confidence and openness, there is ample energy and attention available to focus on achievements and higher sense of purpose. Indeed, Net Gen members are extremely self-aware, concerned with personal growth, fulfilling their potential, and being of service to humanity and the planet.

Calling of Our Times

The aspirations of the newest generation entering our workforce, who will be the leaders of tomorrow, give great hope. Positive psychology provides sound theory about how we can continue to develop such talent. With optimal functioning enabling individuals to live their best lives and to improve well-being and productivity, our families, schools, workplaces, and communities will all be better off. The fusion of this tech-savvy generation and the growth of positive psychology focusing on human strengths and optimal well-being can serve to expedite flourishing communities and workplaces.

What the world is calling for is much clearer than it has ever been. We have started to think more consciously of ensuring the future for generations to come. There is a collective groundswell to serve. In the first decade of the 21st century, the world really did change. The citizens of this planet reached a tipping point in just about every domain, resulting in more people speaking up for greater compassion and understanding across cultures; workers and shareholders alike calling for greater transparency and integrity in financial markets; consumers seeking products and services that conserve our natural resources and health. Alongside these positive seismic systemic shifts, our communication channels and flows became easier, faster, and more far-reaching, collaborative, and compassionate. Out of curiosity, and in many cases necessity to make sense of our world, more and more of us, and particularly the Net Generation, are connecting to people of other cultures in far lands. We find these connections to be sources of great innovation and inspiration, putting us in touch with our own creativity and imaginations. Social media, including networks, wikis, blogs, podcasts, and video, bring us together as one world. We increasingly self-select into online communities in which we are finding mutual interests, shared passions, connection points, and a sense of belonging. Our films and entertainments have become increasingly multi- and cross-cultural. We laugh together. We cry together. We celebrate our global humanity.

There is exciting energy around renewed optimism, hope, and possibility, spreading virally through the sharing of new ideas—some established and many radical—and the creation of new knowledge through collaboration on the World Wide Web and through other social media tools. As if in harmonious alignment with these new and innovative ways of interacting in and with the world, positive psychology, strengths-based approaches and methodologies such as Appreciative Inquiry are perfectly timed to help us make sense of all that we are experiencing at this time in history. These approaches reconnect us with the best of who we are from the philosophical, psychological, and spiritual dimensions.

Overview of Appreciative Inquiry and Positive, Strength-Based Approaches to Human and Organization Development

PART II PROVIDES an overview of Appreciative Inquiry, positive psychology, and two strength-based approaches. Synergistically, they contribute significantly to the field of human and organization development.

A Symphony of Strengths

"What if strengths connected to strengths had the power to help us not merely perform but to transform?" David Cooperrider posed this question in his opening keynote at The Power of Positive Change Conference in 2007. At this ground-breaking conference, David Cooperrider (Appreciative Inquiry), Martin Seligman (positive psychology), and Marcus Buckingham (strength-based management) came together with other leaders in this expanding field of human and organization development to celebrate, share, and learn more about the fusion of Appreciative Inquiry, positive psychology, and strength-based management. All three disciplines are branches on the same trajectory, with their focus on positive institutions, elevating well-being, and human strengths. In the first decade of the 21st century, it seemed the world was calling for new ways of living and working together, and the field of human and organization development had already been offering solutions. Two of Albert Einstein's most popular quotations never seemed more relevant: "No problem can be solved from the same level of consciousness that created it. We must see the world anew" and "There are only two ways to live your life. One as though nothing is a miracle. The other as though everything is a miracle."

While Appreciative Inquiry, positive psychology, and strength-based approaches are three distinct and independent bodies of work, they are intricately interconnected through their shared psychological/ philosophical worldview and practical application that living to our highest potential is achieved more easily and gracefully when we (1) consciously create environments that facilitate strengthening existing talents and attributes; (2) build positive emotions that lead to positive actions; and (3) accept the power of positive imagery on the human psyche to effect the changes we want in our lives. History has shown that a significant factor in human survival is our capacity to imagine a positive future (Cooperrider, 2001). The redirection of attention and investment into what works well in living systems and the image of a positive future redresses the long-held paradigm of first looking backward at weaknesses and deficits as the most effective way to solve problems. With the newer disciplines, we can not only solve problems from a positive perspective in the short term, but also are more likely to improve the overall health and well-being of individuals, families, institutions, and organizations in the long term.

Appreciative Inquiry is positive psychology and strength-based approaches all rolled up into one package. The affirmative change method that is Appreciative Inquiry starts by discovering the healthiest, most positive attributes that already exist in living systems and extends, elevates, and amplifies those attributes and capabilities. Through Appreciative Inquiry's structured process, we become active participants in people's most inspiring stories of optimal human functioning; soon, these stories start meshing to become part of the collective experience. In Appreciative Inquiry, we call the sum total of these positive attributes the "positive core." The positive core comprises the very best attributes of living systems and, in organizations, examples include successful strategies and experiences, existing knowledge and wisdom, loyal customers, exemplary products and services, skills and behaviors, brand identity, reputation, processes and systems, leadership, values, vision and so on. When people or organizations tune into their positive core, they not only connect with their strengths and talents, they also ignite their positive emotions and expand their thinking and their actions to include new possibilities.

An overview of Appreciative Inquiry and its overlaps with positive psychology and strength-based approaches will increase facilitators' knowledge and thereby enhance your credibility, enjoyment. and delivery of the workshops in Part III, thus creating a positive and productive experience for the participant. While I provide a basic introduction to the principles, process, and practice that underpin Appreciative Inquiry, you will most likely hunger for more. There seems to be a consistent pattern: those who are attracted to this worldview—this way of working and being in the world—intuit its power immediately. "It makes such good sense," is the most frequent comment I hear. "Why wouldn't people want to find out what makes them perform at their best and be the most helpful resource possible to themselves and to others?"

Appreciative Inquiry

Appreciative Inquiry came onto the scene in the 1980s. David Cooperrider, then a doctoral student at Case Western Reserve University, in Cleveland, Ohio, undertook action research at the Cleveland Clinic. In analyzing the data, he was struck with the positivity generated when people were performing well together. Levels of cooperation and innovation were higher than usual. His advisor, Suresh Srivastva, suggested he shift the focus of his research to study factors that contribute to optimal group functioning. The board of the clinic was so encouraged by Cooperrider's initial findings that they invited him to apply this method to their whole organization. This shift in focus from conventional analysis of what was not working in the organization to one of what was working became known as the method of analysis Cooperrider later named Appreciative Inquiry. "More than a method or technique, the appreciative mode of inquiry was described as living with, being with, and directly participating in the life of a human system in a way that compels one to inquire into the deeper life-generating essentials and potentials of organizational existence" (Cooperrider, 1990, p. 16).

In the *Appreciative Inquiry Handbook,* Appreciative Inquiry is described as "the cooperative co-evolutionary search for the best in people, their organizations, and the world around them. It involves the discovery of what gives 'life' to a living system when it is most effective, alive and constructively capable in economic, ecological, and human terms" (Cooperrider, Whitney, & Stavros, 2008, p. 3).

In the last thirty years, much has been written about Appreciative Inquiry as an organization development and innovative change method from the academic perspective, and thousands of cases studies are written up and published online and off-line, describing its applications in health, education, human services, faith-based, non-government organizations, non-profits, community building, communities of practice, and multinational corporations. In the last ten years, books have come out that document the new applications of Appreciative Inquiry in a variety of contexts and fields, beyond organization development, for strengthening all kinds of relationships—from marriage guidance to raising children, to dealing with illness, grieving, coaching, team building, and leadership. *Appreciative Inquiry for Collaborative Solutions* is a practical book to help the "doers" in organizations facilitate conversations on important topics that lead to faster collaborative mindsets that will not only improve performance, but transform performance and, furthermore, begin to shift organization cultures to strength-based.

Appreciative Inquiry is a change method and, as a change method, it is first and foremost an *inquiry* into what already works well before any change is introduced. This form of inquiry invites people to dialogue and make meaning together around a specific topic or agenda. The tone remains conversational during the inquiry. There is a structure to the inquiry called the 4-D Cycle. The 4-D's are *discovery, dream, design,* and *destiny.* Detailed descriptions of each are included later in this section. In the *discovery* phase of the inquiry, participants conduct paired interviews in order to learn what is already known about the topic of the inquiry. The interviewer and interviewee enter into a joint discovery through the telling of their own stories in relation to the topic of the inquiry. The state of mind that works best during the inquiry is one of curiosity. The term *appreciative* describes the mode of the inquiry: the inquiry is conducted with a valuing lens, an appreciative eye. Appreciative Inquiry surfaces universal, transcendental values: the good, the true, and the beautiful in living systems. The deliberate choice of affirmative language and artful design has people not only connecting to peak experiences in sharing their stories with others, but also anticipating a future filled with inspiring possibilities. "Appreciation is the mental strength that allows a leader to consciously peer into the life-giving present, only to find the future brilliantly interwoven in the texture of the actual" (Cooperrider, 1990, p. 18).

Inquire

Inquire, verb

1. the act of exploration and discovery

2. to ask questions; to be open to seeing new potential and possibilities

Synonyms: Discovery, search and systematic exploration, study

Source: Cooperrider, Whitney, & Stavros, 2008, p. 275

Appreciate

Appreciate, verb,

1. valuing; the act of recognizing the best in people or the world around us; affirming past and present strengths, successes, and potentials; to perceive those things that give life (health, vitality, excellence) to living systems

2. to increase in value, e.g. the economy has appreciated in value

Synonyms: Valuing, prizing, esteeming, and honoring

Source: Cooperrider, Whitney, & Stavros, 2008, p. 275

Creating Stakeholder Value

Living and doing business in a multi-stakeholder world, we understand increasingly our need to create value for all the stakeholders: those internal to the organization and those external, including families, customers, suppliers, communities in the area, shareholders, agencies, and so on. Our global interdependencies and our dynamic connections have become so much more obvious over the last twenty years. The value of Appreciative Inquiry, as a change method, becomes more apparent as it works to connect and engage all those (internal and external) with some stake in the system. Its design provides the structure for everyone to contribute to the affirmative topic of inquiry, in an honoring way, beginning with one-on-one interviews and climaxing with empowered individuals speaking up, declaring their commitment to actions that will positively impact the organization.

The factor that makes Appreciative Inquiry successful is its solutions-focused design. This focus on that which *we want* (versus *don't want*) is facilitated within a positive framework, accessing the healthiest and most successful moments, mobilizing people to action through their positive images of the future. These principles and practices put vitality and passion back into organizing. Amplifying human virtuousness and financial profitability can co-exist: a healthy reminder for all business transactions.

The Principles of Appreciative Inquiry

A basic overview of the five core principles is necessary to understand why Appreciative Inquiry works its magic the way it does. Organizations, according to Appreciative Inquiry theory, are centers of human relatedness more likely to flourish where there is an appreciative eye: when people see the best in one another, when they explore their concerns and aspirations in affirming ways, when they are connected in full voice to create not just new worlds but better worlds. Over the years as the methodology has evolved, other Appreciative Inquiry practitioners have contributed additional principles, which are equally as relevant and significant. For an excellent comprehensive description of the five core principles and the emerging ones, I recommend Jackie Bascobert Kelm's, *Appreciative Living*.

The five core principles are as follows:

- *Constructionist Principle:* Words create worlds
- *Principle of Simultaneity:* The very first question starts the change
- *Poetic Principle:* What we focus on grows
- *Anticipatory Principle:* Image inspires action
- *Positive Principle:* Positive affect leads to positive action

Each is described in more detail below.

Constructionist Principle: Words Create Worlds

This principle emphasizes the role of language and places human communication and conversation at the center of human organizing and change. As people converse and create meaning together, they sow the seeds for action. Our realities are created in communication with others, and knowledge is generated through social interaction. If the conversation during a tea break is filled with uplifting stories of success, you are likely to contribute your own story of success and all of you will walk away having expanded your understanding of success, building on each other's ideas.

For example, let's say you have been asked to facilitate a workshop on customer complaints. You could pull a group together and say: "We need to do an analysis of customer complaints." Or you could invite them to inquire into stories of "delighting the customer." The latter is more likely to open us up to new ways of knowing. A much quoted statement about the Constructionist Principle is, "The way of knowing is fateful" (Cooperrider, Whitney, & Stavros, 2008, p. 8).

As we become more conscious of the language we use, the conversations we take part in, and the stories we tell ourselves, we notice how they impact and shape us. For this reason, if we seek to change the culture, we need to change the language we use and the stories we tell ourselves and others. Words create worlds.

Principle of Simultaneity: The Very First Question Starts the Change

This principle makes us aware that, as change agents, leaders, facilitators, or as parents, the very first question we ask starts the change process. The way we ask the questions determines what we find. It provides a moment of choice. Inquiry and change are simultaneous. The practice of Appreciative Inquiry involves the art of crafting and asking questions that elicit possibility and inspire images of the future. We need to consider the direction of the question. Is it life depleting or life nurturing?

For example, we are likely to receive different responses from the following two questions: (1) How was work today? and (2) What's the best thing that happened at work today? The first question usually elicits a response such as "OK," "Not bad," or "Fine." It may not always be the answer, but often it is. The second question focuses the attention on "the best thing that happened" and the conversation opens up and will head in a totally different direction. There is also a different energy experienced in the two different responses. The first one is likely to be neutral, and the second one is likely to be more energized.

Poetic Principle: What We Focus on Grows

This principle states that the topics or subjects we choose to put our attention to or study are fateful in the sense that they not only determine what we learn, but they actually create it. Each of us has our own experiences and interpretations that we bring to a topic or conversation. Just as if we were to look at a piece of art, watch a movie, read a poem, or listen to music, there are opportunities for endless learning, interpretations, and inspiration. The metaphors we use shape our beliefs. Is our workplace likened to a machine, a garden, a web, a family, a school, a prison, or a zoo? Through our Appreciative Inquiry lens, we consciously seek out that which we want more of, not less—hence what we focus on grows. There are many examples of this principle in all walks of life, from raising children, to evaluating employee performance, to attending to health and wellness. Do we place our attention and energy on the behaviors and results we want to see in our children, co-workers, and diet and exercise regimes in order to create that which we desire or do we place our attention on the things we want less of? When we place sincere effort on the attributes we want to see and can let go of those that do not serve or support, we have greater chance of success at achieving our desired outcomes.

Anticipatory Principle: Image Inspires Action

This principle speaks to the power of vision, especially the ability to create and hold the vision of the future that we want to bring into the world. Organizations, countries, and communities exist, in part, because people are drawn to and share images and projections of the future. Success or failure can be strongly influenced by the images we hold. Fear-based and deficit-based cultures take off in one way, and cultures of trust and generosity in another. The images we hold of ourselves and others are played out in our daily interactions and in our relationships. If we hold an image of an abundant world of generosity and kindness, our motivations and interactions will be very different from holding an image of scarcity and deprivation. The stories we tell ourselves are fulfilled. Stories of success and pride evoke success and pride. Our ability to dream and imagine positive futures is woven into our history.

For example, think about an important event coming up: it could be a vacation, a business trip, a wedding, a presentation, a medical procedure, or a birth. Whatever the event, you will be filled with anticipation. You will have images that you project into the future of how this event coming up could be. You could anticipate your future event with dread and loathing, fearing the worst, doubting your success, worrying about the possibility of things going wrong or not as you hope. You could also anticipate your future event with love, tranquility, or excitement and joy, imagining success and positive results. Our imaginations are powerful and fuel our thoughts and actions. We choose what kinds of images we fill our heads with. By changing our images of the future we can change our future. This is why language is so important in setting in motion the supportive, positive triggers that lead to desired outcomes. "Yes, we can" sends a very different message from "That won't work." The former directs attention to possibility and the latter to stuckness. Much quoted Henry Ford said it most directly: "Whether you think you can, or you think you can't, either way you're right."

Positive Principle: Positive Affect Leads to Positive Action

This principle reminds us that, when we feel positive, we are more likely to act positively. We see evidence of the benefits that positivity and close social connection bring to groups when people come together to create mutually beneficial solutions both in good times and bad. This principle speaks to the research that shows how positive emotions contribute to our health, resiliency, and optimal functioning. For example, when we expect good performance, we are likely to find it, and when we are acknowledged for good performance, we are more likely to continue to strive to do as well again, if not even better. The Positive Principle speaks to the need for large amounts of positive focus through deliberate choice of language and affirmative questions to discover the most uplifting stories that inspire possibility thinking and thriving futures. The higher the positive affect, the better able we are to deal with the unknown and be more accepting of change than if our positive affect is lower—it is the glass half-full versus the glass half-empty scenario.

As examples illustrating how affirmative language and questions help put folks into resourceful, positive states, consider which of the two questions in the pairs below would help achieve such an objective.

- What are your weaknesses that you need to work on? or What are your strengths that you can develop further?
- Why do we have so many power outages? or How can we ensure uninterrupted power supply?

More about the role of positive emotions will be explained in the section on Positive Psychology.

The Process of Appreciative Inquiry

To reiterate, Appreciative Inquiry, as a change methodology, is a strength-based, generative approach to organization development and behavior, which starts the change process from the affirmative. This differs from the traditional approach, which zeros straight in on the problem, so prevalent in our organizations, institutions, and families. The flow of Appreciative Inquiry, called the 4-D Cycle, is as follows (and is illustrated in Figure 2.1):

- *Discover*—high-point experiences and identify strengths and capabilities—all of which add up to the "positive core."

- *Dream*—imaginatively and collectively envision what else is possible.

- *Design*—co-construct what can be done to build capacity (practically) and what should be done (morally).

- *Destiny*—commit to the iterative exploration of learning, innovation, and delivering results all stakeholders care about.

FIGURE 2.1

4-D Cycle Overview

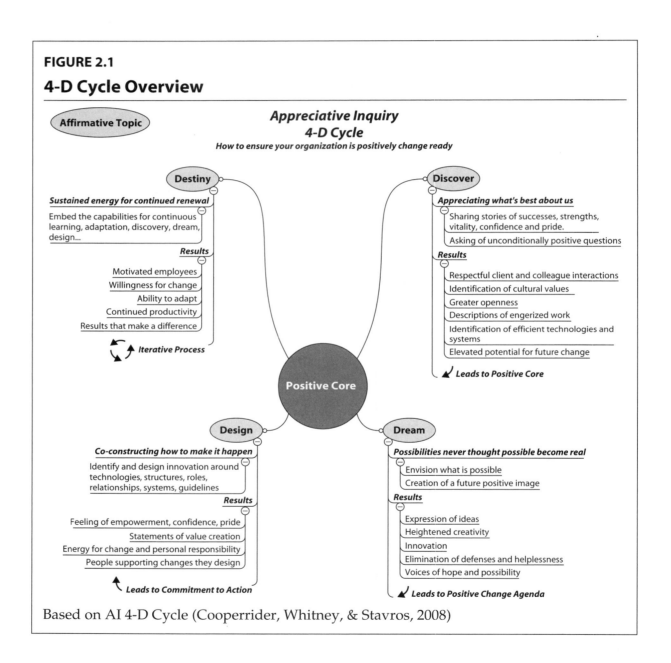

Based on AI 4-D Cycle (Cooperrider, Whitney, & Stavros, 2008)

The *purpose, task,* and *deliverables* associated with each step are described below.

Discover

Purpose: To discover and appreciate the best of "what is" through discovering personal and organizational high-point stories and experiences, highlighting strengths, assets, and successes.

Task: Through paired interviews, participants conduct an inquiry into the chosen topic to gather stories and key ideas. These stories will be examples of the healthiest moments that identify the system's "positive core."

Deliverables: The stories are overflowing with evidence of what has worked in the past; what participants value about the situation, themselves, their colleagues, and organizations—as told through their own stories. The discovery interview results in a deepened ability to listen respectfully; greater openness and opportunity to enhance trust among members; identification of cultural values; descriptions of energized and engaged work; examples of successful technologies, systems, and processes; increased knowledge of individual and organizational capabilities; and elevated potential for future change. All these positive attributes make up the positive core of the organization.

Dream

Purpose: To co-create a desired future for the organization from the collective, imaginative, and innovative capacity of the group based on past successes, current strengths, and future possibilities.

Task: Participants playfully and imaginatively co-create visions of a desired future "what might be"—including all those elements they want to introduce into their workplaces or communities, which they now know is possible, because of what they discovered in the previous step and identified as their positive core.

Deliverables: Clear statements and images of what the organizational members want to see in their idealized organization of the future that are feasible, motivating, and possible. Creativity is heightened as ideas are enthusiastically expressed and innovation is amplified as voices of hope and possibility diminish defensive and helpless thoughts and behaviors. These dream statements are the foundation for the positive change agenda.

Design

Purpose: To choose the design elements that will support and develop the organizational, social, technological, and fiscal infrastructures to help manifest the dream. Design elements include structure, systems, policies, processes, roles, technologies, relationships, leadership, brand, reputation—both operational and strategic, depending on the expertise of participants.

Task: Participants identify which projects they want to sign up for to make the dream happen. Projects will be a combination of what to keep doing because it already serves; what can be phased out because it no longer serves; and what new innovations can be introduced to support emerging markets, trends, and so on.

Deliverables: Rudimentary project plans to be submitted for consideration and refinement. This step is the beginning of sustained commitment to action. Other outcomes include shifts in behaviors and mindsets toward projects the participants themselves create and toward each other. There is evidence of increased personal pride, confidence, and empowerment.

Destiny

Purpose: To sustain momentum in the organization so members build the capacity to keep doing it for themselves with an *appreciative eye*.

Task: Participants, through learning and adapting, pay attention to the iterative nature of the 4-D cycle. Possibility thinking and looking for opportunities and solutions over problem identification and analysis is continuously reinforced and rewarded.

Deliverables: Participants become self-sustaining change champions by continuing to focus on what they want through revisiting the 4-D cycle for renewal, helping to shift the culture of the organization to become strength-based with appreciative practices.

Two important factors distinguish Appreciative Inquiry from other change methods in relation to the 4-D cycle:

- It is the *affirmative topic* of the inquiry that sets the frame and guides the entire agenda.

- The articulation of the *positive core*, which represents the collective attributes, strengths, and assets of the system and remains central and pivotal to the dream, design, and destiny phases in the Appreciative Inquiry process.

The Practice of Appreciative Inquiry

The very first questions we ask, as stated in the Simultaneity Principle, are fateful in that they serve to guide the direction of the inquiry and the stories that are subsequently told. In an organizational context, they ultimately determine the change direction for the organization. With Appreciative Inquiry, the art of asking unconditionally positive questions strengthens the system's capacity to anticipate positive potential toward change. In applying the principles, we know that:

- We live in a world our questions create.
- Change begins with the very first question we ask.
- Our questions determine the results we get.
- The more positive our question, the more it will create the possible.
- Our questions create movement and change.

The question sets or interview protocols, as we call them in Appreciative Inquiry, are designed to elicit the participants' best past stories relating to the inquiry topic and ignite positive energy and enthusiasm for change. Accessing positive emotions helps people remember the best of the past and, with imaginations fired up, they realize it is totally possible and feasible to transition the best of the past into the future. Through the affirming questions, the participants co-construct their realities, create new knowledge, and start to generate ideas about how they might apply this new collective knowledge wisely.

Part IV provides details on designing an Appreciative Inquiry experience, including topic selection, question protocols, working with the positive core, designing project plans, and how to maintain momentum during the Destiny phase. Suffice to say here that *destiny* is the iterative process of strengthening the whole system's affirmative capability, enabling it to build hope and momentum around a purpose and embedding processes for learning and adjustment. Appreciative Inquiry, as a participatory change method, is designed so the organizational members own the initiative. Those who are involved and affected need to be included, as the plans, the events, and the future belong to them.

Positive Psychology

Positive psychology became a distinct branch of psychology in 1998 when Martin Seligman, who had just been voted president of the American Psychological Association (APA), determined that positive psychology would be the new charter for the professional body. Seligman convened an illustrious group of academics in the field of psychology, including Ed Diener and Mihaly Czikszentmihalyi, to birth the new charter focusing on the psychology of health, well-being, and happiness. Looking at life from this psychological perspective had not been a formal practice. In fact, in the years following World War II, psychology had become almost singularly focused on treating mental illness. It is referred to as the disease model. The time had come to expand the field to include a well-being model, and it was a conversation with his five-year-old daughter that provided Seligman his Eureka moment, clarifying for him, as the new president of the APA, this new charter. In *Authentic Happiness*, Seligman (2002) shares his personal story in getting to that "aha" moment.

"Raising children, I knew now, was far more than just fixing what was wrong with them. It was about identifying and amplifying their strengths and virtues, and helping them find the niche where they can live these positive traits to the fullest.

"But if social benefits come through putting people in places where they can best use their strengths, there are huge implications for psychology. Can there be a psychological science that is about the best things in life? Can there be a classification of the strengths and virtues that make life worth living? Can parents and teachers use this science to raise strong, resilient children ready to take their place in a world in which more opportunities for fulfillment are available? Can adults teach themselves better ways to happiness and fulfillment?" (Seligman, 2002, pp. 28–29).

In their seminal paper, *Positive Psychology: An Introduction*, Seligman and Csikszentmihalyi describe positive psychology as follows:

"The field of positive psychology at the subjective level is about valued subjective experiences: well-being, contentment, and satisfaction (in the past); hope and optimism (for the future); and flow and happiness (in the present). At the individual level, it is about positive personal traits; the capacity for love and vocation, courage, interpersonal skill, aesthetic sensibility, perseverance, forgiveness, originality, future mindedness, spirituality, high talent and wisdom. At the group level, it is about the civic virtues and the institutions that move individuals toward better citizenship; responsibility, nurturance, altruism, civility, moderation, tolerance, and work ethic" (2000, p. 2).

Just as Appreciative Inquiry adds another perspective and method for solving problems through its innovative design, affirmative language, structure, and process, so too does positive psychology add another lens to the science of psychology by focusing on factors that help individuals, their communities, organizations, and their societies flourish. Both Appreciative Inquiry and positive psychology add to our understanding and knowledge by studying what supports optimal human functioning. They are not discounting the original ways of solving problems and fixing untenable situations: it is not an "either/or" proposition; it is a "both/and." We now have a more holistic way of working with people and their worlds when we shift to a focus that also includes strengths and virtuousness, imaginations and wholeness.

Overview of Positive Psychology

Martin Seligman is called the founding father of positive psychology, and he names Mihaly Csikszentmihalyi as the brains behind it. Csikszentmihalyi and Seligman have been instrumental in engaging young, leading psychologists to focus on improving lives and building human strength and positive resourcefulness. Together with increasing numbers of scientists and psychologists, they continue to add significantly to the research and practice of positive psychology. Happiness, as an object of scientific research, is a major focus because, among other benefits, it can be surveyed, measured, and developed. Seligman classifies happiness in three levels and each level has its own specific skill sets.

1. *The Pleasant Life—pursuit of pleasure.* Our senses and our emotions are at the forefront when we pursue the pleasant life: eating a particular food, smelling a special fragrance, participating in favorite activities with special people, and so on. In the pursuit of pleasure, we learn such skills as amplifying, savoring, showing gratitude, being mindful, and playing. All these skills contribute to the enjoyment of the pleasurable life. Over time, our tastes change and, as we become accustomed to some of the pleasures, they lose their attractiveness and we let them go. An important take-away from the pleasant life is to understand that, while pleasure is fleeting, we can learn to create more pleasurable experiences in our lives, increasing our overall positivity (Fredrickson, 2005, 2009) in turn strengthens our resiliency over time, so we can better deal with unpleasant situations if and when they arise.

2. *The Good Life—pursuit of engagement.* Happiness that we experience in the "Good Life" sense comes from being able to get into a state of flow, being at one with an activity so that time seems to stand still. We are

fully absorbed and feel such concentration with a deep involvement that makes the effort extremely satisfying. It happens at work and at play when we are so highly focused and engrossed that time just flies. Artists and athletes report being in flow or "in the zone" when their bodies and minds become one with the creative or physical act. Observers also report feelings of being in a state of flow, at one with the experience, as, for example, when an orchestra or band plays music so brilliantly that the audience and musicians are transported; or when the football team plays as if every move were choreographed and the crowd is right there with them. The take-aways from the Good Life are that we have greatest chance of living it when we are fully engaged (Csikszentmihalyi, 1990); we are working to our strengths (Clifton & Buckingham, 2001); and we are actively learning, participating in decision making; are respected; and can envision a future in what it is we do (Emery, 1989). Under such conditions, our performance is totally aligned with who we are and who we are becoming (Holzman, 2009).

3. *The Meaningful Life—pursuit of a purpose higher than oneself*. With the Meaningful Life, we are satisfied or happy because we feel we are contributing something that is truly meaningful not only to ourselves but more importantly for others, and it speaks to a larger sense of purpose. Employees report that, when they know their work makes a difference, they are likely to improve their performance. Furthermore, studies coming from The Center for Positive Scholarship (University of Michigan) and anecdotal evidence confirm that organizations performed significantly higher on both hard measures (e.g., financial) and soft measures (e.g., satisfaction) of performance when virtuousness is part of the cultural norm (Cameron, 2004). These findings are supported by the positive growth and attraction of exceptional talent in the non-profit sector, non-governmental organizations (NGO), and socially responsible organizations. When we have passion about what we are doing, our energy is high and we continue to contribute our best, because that's just how it is when an activity is meaningful. Moreover, in such circumstances, our strengths are also at play. The take-away from the Meaningful Life raises questions. What is it that we need to pay attention to as we go about creating a life that has meaning and purpose for each of us? Can we experience happiness that is meaningful without pleasure and engagement? In the work context, is our day-to-day productivity a function of pleasure, engagement, and meaning? How do we make our homes and our workplaces environments that

foster pleasure, engagement, and meaning? In a presentation, which can be viewed on the website TED (www.ted.com), Csikszentmihalyi quotes the first mission statement of the co-founders of the Sony Corporation, created in 1946, as an example that that speaks to all three: "To establish a place of work where engineers can feel the joy of technological innovation, be aware of their mission to society, and work to their heart's content."

Broaden and Build Theory of Positive Emotions

Barbara Fredrickson, who heads up the Positive Emotions and Psychophysiology Laboratory at the University of Chapel Hill, created the "Broaden and Build" theory of positive emotions (Fredrickson, 2001). Her scientific research shows "how our day-to-day emotional experiences affect the very course of our lives" (Fredrickson, 2009, p. 12). Both negative and positive emotions create physiological, cognitive, and behavioral shifts. Her findings document that when people feel positive emotions, there is an opening up versus a shutting down effect. The "broadening" effect describes the cognitive, emotional, and physiological changes we experience when positive emotions are aroused. When we feel positive emotions, we momentarily expand our attention and thinking, and we are more open to receive others and their ideas. Moreover, positivity opens us up to possibility, literally expands our peripheral vision, and opens our veins. Instead of focusing on "me," we become appreciative of others and think more about "we." Positive emotions contribute to our ability to speedily bounce back from stress and can potentially transform us for the better.

The "building" effect is the accumulation of positivity over time. Fredrickson's research indicates there is a ratio of 3:1, which is the tipping point for building our positive emotion reserves. If we can, at minimum, think, talk, and behave three times positive to one time negative, then we are on the way to building emotional resiliency that will help us flourish instead of languish. A key finding of this building effect is that it helps us recover from negativity, stress, or life-threatening situations more quickly. Called the "undo" effect, it means that, faced with adversity, those who have greater positivity reserves, or resiliency, will bounce back and move on: physiologically, their heart rates recover far more quickly, which is much healthier in the short and long term.

In her book, *Positivity*, and on the website, www.positivityratio.com, Fredrickson has tools to help us increase the amount of positivity in our lives. With evidence now that positivity opens us to an expanded worldview and increases our personal and social resources, it seems a worthwhile investment to build our positivity ratio. Frederickson's list of positive emotions includes amused, awe, grateful, hopeful, inspired, interested, joyful, love, proud, and serene.

Positive Image Leads to Positive Action

As long as we have had imaginations, people have lived with dreams, aspirations, hopes, and fears. The notion of self-fulfilling prophecy works both in the positive and the negative. If our goal is to build a happy life in the fullest way that includes pleasure, engagement, and meaning, how much more resourceful it is to focus on positive images rather than negative. A simple and most poignant example comes from the words of Mother Theresa: "Peace begins with a smile."

In health, education, psychotherapy, religion, politics, business, sports, and other fields, there are countless examples wherein positive imagery results in positive outcomes. In the following section, I'll describe several scenarios in which positive imagery delivers positive outcomes. For example, patients with steadfast, positive beliefs can, and do, ignite within themselves a healing response, even if their treatment consists of a sugar pill or some other inert substance. What is even more significant is if, in addition to the "sugar pill," doctors and family members also support the positive beliefs, the results are even more powerful. If we hold positive images and align our efforts, the chances of a positive outcome are higher than if we don't hold those positive images. In medicine, the positive outcome that can result from believing the "medicine" will work is known as the Placebo Effect (Beecher, 1955). Positive imagery can precipitate the effect, supporting the belief (Cooperrider, 1990). That the brain rewires itself when we apply our minds to a practice, belief, or image is among growing bodies of research coming out of well-regarded institutions, such as Harvard Medical School, MIT, the Universities of Wisconsin, California, and others.

For another example, in a school experiment, teachers had been led to believe that students had been ranked as high achievers and low achievers. The high achievers were treated as having "positive image," and the low achievers were treated as having a "negative image." In truth, the two groups were chosen entirely at random. As the study developed, the manipulated expectations of the teachers were fulfilled. Those students who had been labeled with "positive image" performed better than those students in the group labeled "negative image." This particular study in education, begun in 1968, is an example of a self-fulfilling prophecy that goes way back to Ancient Greek mythology—hence the name: The Pygmalion Effect. People's performance can be influenced by the expectation of others. This is a really important awareness to have in developing others, beginning with children right through to working adults.

A fictitious example from playwright George Bernard Shaw's well-known work, *My Fair Lady* is a classic example of the effect of positive image. A linguist, Professor Higgins, had entered into a wager that he would be able to fool London society by creating the expectation that a Hungarian princess would soon be in their midst. He selected Eliza Doolittle, a poor, humble flower girl in Victorian London and, with his skills, transformed her from a cockney "gutter girl" into a Hungarian princess. Even when he declared all bets off and revealed his trickery, those who had been duped refused to accept it. They wanted to believe she was an exquisite, aristocratic Hungarian princess and hence they saw her as such.

What coaches do not use the power of positive image to inspire, energize, and excite their clients to achieve their highest aspirations—whether athletes, dancers, musicians, or executives? They build on strengths and best past performances; they visualize in the greatest detail the goals they are aiming for; they envision the process step by step. In their imaginations, they go through a full emotional and mental rehearsal that alerts the body for performance. They project the images of the future, or run the movie in their heads, over and over. It's what we do. Dewitt Jones, a former photographer with the *National Geographic*, refers to his process of preparing for a photographic shoot. He has learned that, when his expectations were low, he didn't find the scene he was looking for. From experience, he has changed his belief. "When you believe it, you'll see it."

Strength-Based Movement

I will focus on two main camps in the strengths field—the scientific camp (psychology) and the business camp (organization and leadership development)—and how they overlap and how they can be translated into organizational strengths. Their co-mingling and overlapping lend great support to the strengths movement. As mentioned earlier under the positive psychology section, investing in identifying and maximizing one's innate talents or strengths is key to optimizing well-being, human flourishing, and a happy life (with the emphasis on the engagement and meaning aspects of happiness).

There are many instruments, surveys, and indicators that will help individuals assess their strengths from a number of different angles: brain dominance, personality preferences, social styles, and so on. There are also surveys that assess strengths from (1) a character perspective, such as Seligman and Peterson's Values in Action (VIA) Survey of Character and (2) a natural talent perspective, such as Clifton and Buckingham's StrengthsFinder Profile. Both of these are designed to shine the light on our personal strengths, and while they are different, they both use the term "signature strengths." Both are valuable.

To help understand the distinction, here is a very brief overview. Don Clifton, after nearly thirty years of studying excellence in two million people, identified themes that reflected natural talents, naming them signature strengths. He recommends that for success and fulfillment we "capitalize on strengths, whatever they may be, and manage around weaknesses, whatever they may be" (Clifton & Buckingham, 2002, p. 27). He defines strengths as "consistent near perfect performance in an activity ... the ability is a strength only if you can fathom yourself doing it repeatedly, happily, and successfully" (Clifton & Buckingham, 2001, p. 26). Their online survey, StrengthsFinder, identifies talents that are the greatest potential for strength. The five most dominant themes of talent, the authors state, are just that—"themes of talent"—and "may not yet be strengths." There are a total of thirty-four "themes of talent," and the five that are one's highest potential for strength are where one is advised to focus attention for development, because it is with those themes where one will find the greatest satisfaction and do what comes most naturally. "By focusing on your top five themes, you will actually become stronger, more robust, more open to new discoveries and, importantly, more appreciative of people who possess themes very different from your own" (Clifton & Buckingham, 2001, p. 144).

The Values in Action (VIA) Survey of Character was created by Chris Peterson of the University of Michigan between 1998 and 2001. The VIA has been available online at www.authentichappiness.com for free since 2001. It measures twenty-four character strengths, identifying the dominant top five, which are most core to a respondent's character. With knowledge of one's character strengths, it is possible to articulate and develop character and be poised to better direct talents and abilities into meaningful and engaging behavior to improve one's own life and the lives of others. The belief is that your top five strengths are one's signature strengths and when we work with them and strengthen them in all aspects of our lives, we lead a life that engages us fully and is meaningful. When we are working to our strengths, we feel authentic, excited and at ease, invigorated, productive and enterprising. The evidence for these states is that we learn far more quickly when we have a talent for something; we gain greater satisfaction when we perform to our natural talents; and we experience a desire or a yearning to perform the activity, as we feel we just have to do it (Seligman, 2002).

Clifton's StrengthsFinder Profile and Peterson's VIA Character Strengths help individuals identify their strengths, offering valuable insights and development opportunities. They both facilitate people to become more consciously aware of their best selves—what energizes them so they perform with ease or what depletes them so they find themselves struggling; which environments stimulate them or bore them; which behaviors calm them or excite them. Over time, this adds up to a life that is efficient, effective, healthy, productive, and satisfying.

Implications and Applications

So what do you do with this abundance of talent and all these strengths—character and potential—that have been identified in your organization? How do you capitalize on strengths linked to strengths? I am again reminded of David Cooperrider's opening question at the Symphony of Strengths Conference in 2007: "What if strengths connected to strengths had the power to help us not merely perform but to transform?" This is where Appreciative Inquiry as an organization development change method comes into its own and channels the collective strengths toward first discovering, then dreaming, then designing an organization that is "most effective, alive, and constructively capable in economic, ecological, and human terms" (Cooperrider, Whitney, & Stavros, 2008, p. 3).

To recap: Appreciative Inquiry identifies the organization's strengths during the discovery interview when participants identify the "positive core." Strengths are the sum total of all the organization's assets, including individual talents, knowledge, and skills, and its products, services, technologies, customers, processes, systems, reputation, and so on. These collective strengths become the foundation for dreaming and designing the future the organization aspires to. Peter Drucker, in his seminal book *The Effective Executive,* links strengths to organizational effectiveness and success. In an interview with David Cooperrider in 2003, he said, "The task of leadership is to create an alignment of strengths in ways that make the organizations weaknesses irrelevant."

What do strength-based organizations look like? Each of us has a sense of what the answer would be like. It might include any or all of the following: a totally sustainable environment in harmony with nature; state-of-the-art technologies; artwork that compliments the décor; childcare facilities; a large fitness center; meditation and massage areas; subsidized dining facilities; flexible working hours; transparent accounting practices and management practices; participatory and shared leadership; congruency between espoused and in-practice values and principles; ongoing learning and development opportunities; diverse workforce; caring, compassionate, and humane workplace practices; community-minded cultures; respectful relationships; appreciative customers; generous vendors; innovative, leading-edge products and services; an outstanding reputation; really interesting, meaningful work; and a fun place to be.

Some of the above are core to a strength-based organization and some are cosmetic. The core components are an empowered, engaged workforce who knows and appreciates the organization's vision, mission, purpose, direction, strategies, structures, systems, and processes; who have optimal levels of decision-making and autonomy; who have optimal learning opportunities; and whose work includes optimal variety so they remain interested and involved. In addition, employees are looking for maximum amounts of respect, knowing the meaning and value of their contributions to the whole and able to see they have a future (Emery, 1989). All of this implies that employees are in roles that match their talents. Furthermore, the culture of the organization is one that Frank Barrett articulates as demonstrating "consistent strength in four key kinds of competence: affirmative, expansive, generative and collaborative" (Cooperrider, 2003, p. 181). Figure 2.2 summarizes the attributes of these four organizational competencies.

Questions you might pose in relation to your organization's readiness to embrace a strength-based culture include the following:

- *Affirmative Competence*—What are some ways your organization can develop this competence (actions, procedures, policies, leadership styles, management practices, etc.)?

- *Expansive Competence*—How would you inspire members to feel excited about stepping outside the box from time to time? What are some innovations you know would expand the organization's capacity?

- *Generative Competence*—What helpful methods, resources, and technologies would allow members to keep informed of their progress and let them know how their work contributions are received, make a difference, and/or add value to the whole?

- *Collaborative Competence*—What recommendations do you have to develop this competence so that people work in support of each other, complement each other, and have real dialogue about what's going on at the local and global levels?

FIGURE 2.2

Appreciative Inquiry Organizational Competencies

- **Affirmative Competence**
  - Recognition of past successes, achievements, valuing members' strengths and vitality

- **Expansive Competence**
  - Willingness to stretch the boundaries, take on challenges for growth, expand to new and different horizons, inspire members

- **Generative Competence**
  - Meaning making and sense-making is built into performance; timely feedback and progress reports to acknowledge members' contributions

- **Collaborative Competence**
  - High performing organizations allow for dialogue, encourage diversity and multiple perspectives and all members' participation in the service of the goals

---

With the evidence amassing over the last thirty years of the power to create positive, sustainable change in people, cultures, and organizations and the planet, a constant key predictor of peak performance and sustained commitment remains the ability to create an environment in which people are engaged and energized. Each of the twenty-one workshops in Part III of this book provides that opportunity. Each topic starts conversations that will move your organization closer to becoming a strength-based culture.

Part III

Collaborative Workshops

Introduction

This part of the book is divided into two sections: the first contains guidelines and recommendations for using the workshops, and the second contains twenty-one workshops on a range of affirmative topics to introduce positive, strength-base change.

The guidelines and recommendations will help you, the facilitator, do the best job for your participants and yourself. We review the workshops' design principles and facilitation practice: the importance of affirmative topics and language; the fateful role of the first questions; the significance of positive imagery leading to positive actions; group dynamics; being clear about workshop objectives and learning outcomes; understanding where you are in the 4-D cycle; and stepping back to allow the collective sense-making to emerge from the group.

The workshops cover a range of topics. Some are oldies but goodies—those that are always in demand; for example, change, leadership, team building, creativity, and customer service. Then there are newer topics that are of growing strategic importance as generational shifts (demographic as well as technological) influence us with unprecedented speed—topics such as collaboration, diversity, social media, environment, sustainability, and life/work balance, to name a few. The topics, process, and structure of each workshop are designed following the Appreciative Inquiry 4-D Cycle, leaving the specific contextual content to be determined by the facilitator and the participants.

All twenty-one workshops enable participants to discover existing strengths and assets through generative conversations that accelerate the rate at which people find connection and make sense of the collective inputs. As participants find meaning together and co-create new knowledge, they amplify and elevate the strengths and assets of the system—the "positive core" and, as a result, feelings and expressions of self and group empowerment are palpable.

Workshop Design Principles

As previously stated, to change the culture of an organization, the narrative of the organization needs to change, as the stories we tell ourselves are those that guide our beliefs and choices, thereby impacting our actions. The design of Appreciative Inquiry questions accesses positive emotional states, because when we are in positive emotional states, we are more creative, playful, inclusive of others, and open to possibility (Fredrickson & Branigan, 2005). Coupled with positive feeling is the power of positive image. Studies of individuals and cultures show that holding a positive image of the future has greater likelihood of increasing our positive thoughts, which lead to positive actions (Cooperrider, 1990; Fredrikson, 2005). So remembering and recounting past high-peak experiences, as participants experience in the first discovery interview, they access positive feelings, which further increases positive, resourceful states and enables them to more expansively imagine a future they want to be part of. In Appreciative Inquiry, we experience the future we aspire to in the dream phase of the 4-D cycle.

Workshop Practice: What You Can Expect

These workshops are entirely interactive. Your role as facilitator is to lead the participants through the introductory section of each workshop. Gradually, the participants take on leadership as they share stories, identify themes, and collectively discover what contributes to their best performances. Through story telling, different perspectives open up and new levels of understanding are reached. People begin to make sense of complex issues, and together they create new knowledge. You hold the space for learning, creating a safe environment to allow the process of self-discovery and collective sharing of wisdom to emerge from the participants so that they "own" their content and their solutions. Remember, we support what we create and, as Meg Wheatley writes in her concluding poem in *Turning to One Another*, "There is no power greater than a community discovering what it cares about" (2002, p. 145). Every single person has something to add to a topic. Formerly, we relied on experts to lead us through their maze of methods to the unknown. Our world is changing fast. We all have access to information and have experiences that extend way outside our immediate environments, which potentially add enormous value to any discussion. The design of the question sets in the workshops take participants on a learning journey of discovery, revealing the most empowering stories and experiences. Once they openly share their best performances and experiences, participants build on existing strengths, envision what more is possible, and can then begin to co-create new ways of being together. What follows is a willingness to commit to a shared destiny that can be sustained through iterative cycles of discovery, dreaming, designing, and being open to continue the cycle.

To summarize, we start with the mindset that every participant has some prior experience or knowledge of the topic and, therefore, can contribute. We do this through sharing stories of best experiences in relation to the topic of inquiry. We seek to discover what those prior experiences are and value them for what they are. The process is designed to encourage real conversation; the question sets with all their prompts are mere guides to open up a conversational tone and genuine curiosity. Remember, as a facilitator, you need to allow adequate time for real conversation to emerge so that the participants begin to see each other in an expanded way. The questions are framed affirmatively to focus on what has worked already to access positive emotional states to identify what contributes to people doing best work and, aligned to that, uncover the system's strengths. The strengths become the foundation for an imagined future. Furthermore, the power of positive imagery, and the will to dream a(n) (im)possible dream, is life changing!

Workshop Titles: Affirmative Topics

Notice that the workshop titles are affirmative in their language, evoking movement toward *what we want*. The titles of the workshops are a departure from the conventional way of dealing with change. A key way to shift your organization to a strength-based culture is to reframe problems as opportunities. Traditionally, the titles of many workshops are expressed in deficit language, putting the focus on the issue we want to avoid. With Appreciative Inquiry we focus on what we want to create—the solution itself. In accordance with the principles and practices of our methodology, the stories that are told in organizations and communities are those that we repeat over and over until we believe them at an unconscious and conscious level. These stories are not true in all cases at all times. So if we want to change the stories, we need to change the narrative. The changed narrative will change the culture. If we study deficiencies, weaknesses, gaps, and low morale, that is what we will find. Equally, if we inquire into stories of pride, strengths, successes, and heightened engagement, that is what we will find. Having evidence of that which we want makes the goal far more feasible, motivating, and realizable. So topic choice and the language focus the outcomes. We create that which we focus on. The topics of inquiry shown in Table 3.1 illustrate the differences between affirmative topics and more traditional, deficit-based topics. You can see that the affirmative language is more likely to lead to a generative conversation and changed perspective.

TABLE 3.1

Topics of Inquiry

Affirmative Topic	Traditional Title
Valuing Time	Time Management
Creating Change Positively	Change Management
Respectful Relationships	Conflict Management
Peak Performance	Performance Management
Positive Cross-Gender Relationships	Sexual Harassment
Magnetic Customer Connections	Customer Complaints
Exceptional Arrival Experience	Lost Baggage Complaints
Stories of Passionate Enthusiasm	Low Morale

Purpose of the Workshops

The purpose of each workshop is to work toward a solution through the collaborative process, appreciating multiple perspectives on issues, learning about strengths, and finding shared values, all of which will contribute to the most feasible and motivating outcomes for all. The difference between these workshops and others is that we approach topics from a valuing and strength-based perspective that will move us closer to the goal we want to achieve. The very first question we ask sets the tone and begins the change process. We ask what has worked in the past, what the high points of people's experiences are, which enables them to access their best and proudest selves. Contrast this with "We have a problem here and we need to do a root cause analysis to fix it." We choose to ask instead, "What worked well and what contributed to the success?"

The aim is to consolidate the shared experiences so that we can

- Find the leverage points and the momentum to keep doing that which works;
- Agree on what we need to change or stop doing;
- Identify what we need to create anew; and
- Ensure we are moving toward what we want and can commit to.

Objectives of the Workshops

There are two sets of overarching objectives for the workshops.

1. *Individual or Micro Level:* As a result of participating, individuals will have
   - Increased awareness of personal, collective, and organizational strengths related to the topic of inquiry;
   - Heightened sense of personal responsibility involved in shifting the dialogue to what can be done versus what can't be done; and
   - Contributed toward future steps that will progress the collective imagining of what's possible.

2. *Organizational or Macro Level:* These workshops are an entry point to help organizations become more conscious and strength-based. The participatory affirming way of sharing stories open us up to new ways of living and working. The workshops are a practical way to:
   - Surface mental models;
   - Hold generative conversations;
   - Co-create new meaning from collective knowledge;
   - Experience reflective consciousness; and
   - Work at strengthening the organization's strengths.

In preparing to deliver a workshop, you will probably have some additional, specific objectives in mind and an idea of desired workshop outcomes, based on the learning needs of your group and your organization.

Workshop Selection

It is most likely you will select a workshop based on the strategic or learning need that is important to the community at the time. Table 3.2 illustrates two examples of workshop selection based on the presenting need and the solution sought.

There is flexibility within each workshop, as the affirmative topic can address a number of issues. Your context and your organization's need will determine how each affirmative topic can be interpreted, thus shaping the workshop's objectives and its outcomes. Moreover, as facilitator, you might like to tweak some of the focus to suit your own constituents. These workshops provide you with a solid, proven framework, and if you need to customize one, it is easy to do.

TABLE 3.2

Selecting a Workshop

Presenting Need: Problem you are asked to solve	Training Solution: Select an appropriate workshop to help address the need and deliver the outcomes you aspire to.
Your organization is updating technology systems and you are asked to *"deal with negative attitudes about the changes."*	Any one of the following workshops will help participants shift their perspectives toward change and even identify value in updating to newer technology systems. • Creating Change Positively • Valuing Technology • Global Interconnectivity
For the first time, there are four generations working together. Their differences cause tensions and loss of productivity. You are asked to *"do something to reduce the tension causing loss of productivity."*	Any one of the following workshops will help participants see one another's perspectives and value difference. • Generations Working Together • Flourishing Communities • Nurturing Diversity

Workshop Duration and Participant Selection

The workshops vary in length, but are typically between two and a half and four hours. There are recommended time allocations for the activities, and you will decide how long you might need to complete a workshop depending on the issues you are dealing with, the mix of participants, and your own style. A most important consideration is to ensure you complete the workshop in the time you allocate so you reach a satisfying stopping point for everyone.

The workshops are relevant to everyone in an organization. If you can gather totally diverse groups, your organization and its members will obtain maximum value out of all the different perspectives on an issue. The process and topics are as relevant to intact teams as they are to cross-sections of the organization—horizontally and vertically. I personally prefer to have senior executives attend with less experienced members, as each learns so much from the other, listening to different stories, dreams, and solutions to issues. As facilitator, you respond to the organization's need to develop capability related to the topic of inquiry. The topic might be specific to one team to explore and resolve together, or it may be relevant across the organization.

Structure of Content

All workshops are designed with a flow incorporating elements of the Appreciative Inquiry 4-D Cycle of Discover, Dream, Design, and Destiny. (Refer to Figure 2.1.)

Discovery Phase

The affirmative questions in the *discovery interview* have participants very quickly engaged in telling their stories of high-point experiences in relation to the topic of the inquiry. Common themes emerge from the stories that become part of the collective experience and contribute to the organization's "positive core." The positive core is made up of those qualities, attributes, strengths, and assets that already exist in the system, all of which will take the organization into the future, provide continuity, and be a source of pride and confidence to each participant. The turning point is discovering in the present moment a future possibility from a place of knowing you have succeeded in the past.

The first part of the Appreciative Inquiry–based workshop, the *discovery interview* is a time when participants are working in pairs interviewing each other in a quiet, respectful tone, listening, talking, clarifying, and taking notes. When the interviews are complete, the interview pairs join one or two other interview pairs and share stories. At this point, the conversations become animated and louder.

Dream Phase

The themes identified as the positive core become the inspiration and energy for co-creating what is possible. The *dream* phase builds on the knowledge and insights of the collective strengths and capacities learned in the discovery interviews. It comes from the participants' own grounded realities. The *dream* is a co-creation of a vision born out of the collective imaginative and innovative capacity of the system. During this creative, energizing, playful phase, participants incorporate and leverage their best attributes, with awareness that their strengths are transferable to any change agenda going forward. Change is experienced with an appreciative eye, and participants are energized by what is possible. The potential for transformative change lies in the shift from learned helplessness to learned helpfulness. To expand this notion even more, such activity leads to empowerment and engagement in the moment and beyond.

The energy in the room during the *dream* phase is high, especially if you invite the participants to be as creative as they want and provide them with props, such as colored paper, marker pens, fabrics, toys, and Plasticine®, to create drawings, collages, or skits. It works well to have the whole brain working by bringing in the right side to complement the left from time to time!

Design Phase

Themes and images that come out of the dream phase become agenda items for next steps in the *design* phase, during which participants select those elements that will help construct their dreams of a positive and feasible future. Members *design* the forms of organizing that will serve all stakeholders, produce the desired results, and ensure the work gets done, while in no way compromising the members' highest values and ideals. In other words, it is a combination of what can be done (practically) and what should be done (ethically and morally).

In the collaborative workshops that follow, the *design* phase is most often a collective activity; however, some are individual reflective activities. It depends on the topic and what will serve the outcomes and/or the individual and organization best.

Destiny Phase

Most workshops conclude with a personal declaration about what members will do going forward. Next steps, actions plans, or goals they set become their own form of measurement. They will know whether they deliver on them or not. As facilitator, you can invite the group to determine what else will contribute to sustaining and amplifying the energy and outcomes of the experience. Most often, teams self-organize after an AI session to continue to bring the desired change to life.

Destiny is sustaining the momentum of what the workshop has created. Too often, powerful learning experiences occur, promising relationships are born, trust is felt, positive emotions are elevated, excellent ideas are shared, new knowledge is created, and then all those experiences fail to progress because, once participants leave the room, "work" gets in the way. So *destiny* is how to migrate the new discoveries into "work" and keep the new discoveries alive as part of everyday interactions. *Destiny* is an iterative cycle of *discovery, dream,* and *design*. With follow-up and tools, it becomes possible to move from mere knowing to wise application of our knowing.

Follow-Up

How you go forward is up to you and the participants. You can have ongoing meetings (see Part IV to help you design your own follow-up meetings) or use intranet sites, wikis, blogs, or other relevant social media tools to continue to contribute to the projects and share learnings and success stories. Continuing to extend and amplify that which has been started is the best way to build an empowered, energized community and an organization that is strength-based.

Facilitation Process

Before facilitating a workshop, read through all the question sets in the chosen workshop and decide how much time to allocate to that particular workshop; then determine how long you will give to each focus area. (There are suggested timeframes, but you should decide what will work best in the situation. Remember, you need to allow adequate time for real conversations to emerge—participants are not simply responding to a survey or questionnaire.) The workshops start with paired interviews for the first sets of questions (see Figure 3.1). Then pairs join other pairs to create groups of four to six (see Figure 3.2). At relevant junctures, you, as facilitator, will call the entire group to come back into a plenary session to check in with everyone and to identify common themes, values, aspirations, and so on (see Figure 3.3). During the course of the workshop, participants build the collective knowledge, leading to new strengthened pathways for personal and collective application and implementation.

For the overall group size, twelve to twenty participants works well, allowing for three to five subgroups of four to six participants. Larger numbers (more than twenty participants) require more time, as there is more information from subgroups to process.

FIGURE 3.1

Paired Configuration

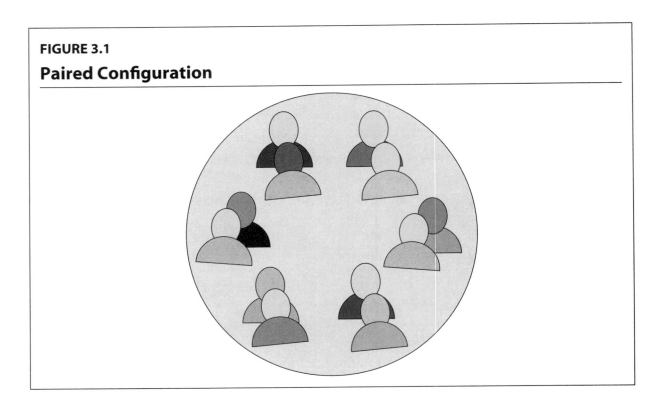

FIGURE 3.2

Small Group Clusters

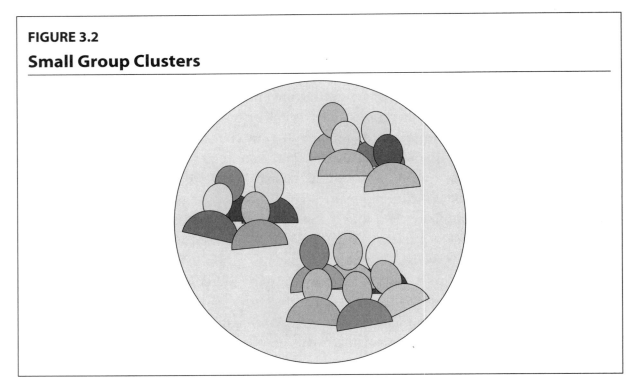

FIGURE 3.3

Plenary Configuration

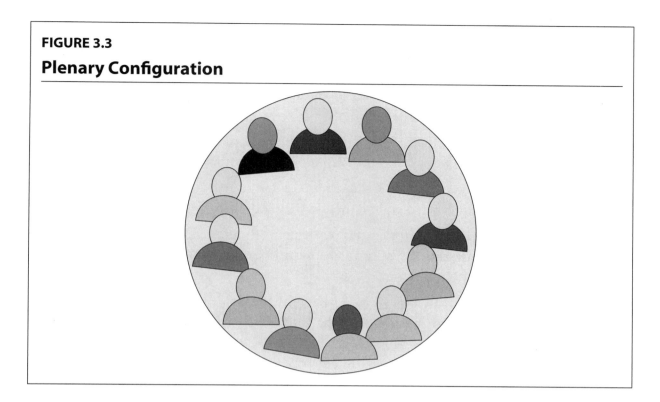

Step-by-Step Process

It will be helpful to read this section while referring to one of the work-shops, so you can envision the setup in relation to the focus and agenda items. Each major step in the workshop agenda is labeled "focus." There are between two and five focus items in each workshop.

Step One: Discovery Interview

1. Distribute copies of the worksheet (which includes the lead-in [intro-ductory] statement and the discussion questions) to all participants and ask them to write their names on the sheets. Participants form pairs and interview each other, reading the lead-in statement and asking all the questions attached to Focus 1. Each interviewer listens and records highlights of the stories on the interviewee's worksheet. This document serves as a record of the interviewee's past successes, values, and strengths.

2. Pairs join one or two other pairs to form clusters of four or six to hear the stories of those in their clusters (Focus 2). Interviewers introduce interviewees to the new members of the group and interviewers share

the high points of the interviewees' stories. In preparation for this step, the facilitator asks the participants to listen for common themes as they hear each other's stories.

3. The clusters of four to six select one story that captures the common themes to share with the whole room.

4. Each cluster reports out to the entire group the one story they have selected that best exemplifies the common themes.

5. The facilitator invites participants to record digitally or on flip-chart paper the common themes they identified in the sharing of stories.

6. The facilitator invites participants to comment on the themes and commonalities across all groups and provide their observations, insights, and learnings.

7. If the insight does not come from the group, the facilitator informs the participants that the attributes, strengths, and assets they have identified comprise the "positive core"—those factors that contribute vitality, aliveness, and energy to the organization when it functions at its best. The facilitator stresses that these are the core strengths of the organization.

Exhibit 3.1 provides an example of the collective themes of a work group after sharing stories of high points on the topic of "Engaging Membership to the Fullest." In this example, there were fifty-eight participants. The group worked through the steps set out above. Upon reaching Step 5, the participants, working in small groups at eight tables, identified the strengths or the "best" examples of when they had experienced *engaged membership to the fullest*. These comments were captured digitally and were streamed and made visible to all participants at the front of the room. The capitalized words are the community strengths or the positive core that the group identified at their tables, namely collaboration, contribution, authenticity, support, learning, fun, diversity, and impact.

What came next was the *dream* phase, projecting into the future how participants envisioned their community in a year's time when these collective strengths were lived out. From the *dream*, they self-selected into working groups around each of the identified strengths to *design* those factors that would bring the dream into reality for them.

EXHIBIT 3.1

Collective High Points of Discovery Interviews and Shared Stories, with Common Themes in All Caps

Question: As you share highlights of your peak experiences, what are your discoveries and collective insights about "membership engaged to the fullest"?

Table Groups	Shared Themes from the Stories Told at Each Table
Table 5	Meet challenges; COLLABORATIVELY CONTRIBUTE in open, receptive environment; personally grow, then enable others to empower themselves; AUTHENTICITY; greater responsibility; emotional engagement feeling part of larger culture and betterment of humanity; asking the right questions; successful outcomes; clarity, cut through confusion; challenge; similarity of people's needs; friendship and business overlap; GIVING/getting SUPPORT
Table 1	Interactions with people; ability to network; flexible structure; volunteer based on interests; opportunity to CONTRIBUTE and LEARN; have FUN; team outings
Table 2	LEARNING and growth; valued for our CONTRIBUTION; inclusion and belonging; significant and important topic or matter; opportunity to build friendship and/or intimacy; enjoyed engaging; play; FUN; enjoyment in the process and event or activity
Table 6	Personal CONTRIBUTION; LEARNING; mutual respect; food; well-organized; sense of accomplishment; clear objectives and agendas; positive attitudes; SUPPORTIVE; SHARING and building on ideas; collaborative
Table 3	Energy-FUN; having IMPACT; making a CONTRIBUTION; community; LEARNING; make a difference; AUTHENTICITY; being heard and respected; COMMITMENT
Table 8	Felt very SUPPORTED in organization, which translated to high level of engagement; likes feeling welcomed; congeniality; opportunities to be creative; LEARNING; enjoyed DIVERSITY of people and work; communities created a sense of validation; openness and informality seen as valuable
Table 4	Leadership; DIVERSITY; personal values; COLLABORATION; validation; insurmountable odds followed by success; personal satisfaction; self-actualization; determination; teamwork; situation bigger than self
Table 7	Engage others; COLLABORATION; autonomy; IMPACT; energy; initiative; risk-taking; seeing results; SHARED credit; energizing; innovation
Overarching Themes:	Significance; importance; COLLABORATION; ability to CONTRIBUTE AUTHENTICITY; FUN; people choose to be present; being valued; making a difference; LEARNING; challenge followed by success; IMPACT; friendship and business overlap; forgiving environment

Step Two: Dream—Desirable Future

Participants remain in their small group clusters to envision a future they aspire to, based on their discoveries from Step One (Discovery), incorporating their positive core.

The clusters work through all the questions sets attached to Focus 3. As facilitator, you might invite the participants to perform their inspiring future scenarios in creative ways, such as creating a poem, performing a skit, singing a song, or drawing a picture. (Prepare in advance for how you would like the groups to represent their desired futures, so you have the right tools for them.) Decide when it's time to invite the groups to reconvene in a plenary session to share their desirable future scenarios. Your decision to reconvene the groups will be mostly likely driven by time (having determined in advance how much time you allocate to each of the focus areas). Your decision could also be that you can see the participants have come to a place at which they are ready to come back together to share their *dreams*. In some workshops, participants prepare a future possibility statement that is a sentence or two describing their image of the future, not unlike a vision statement. Having a picture of what we want makes it more real and possible. Positive images lead to positive actions.

Step Three: Design and Destiny

This step is usually a call to action. It sometimes involves people self-selecting into work groups or teams to plan projects and action steps; sometimes, it is an individual activity in which the individual reflects on the workshop and determines what he or she is moved to do as a result of the workshop (Focus 4 and, at times, Focus 5). As the facilitator, you invite reflection and sharing as you deem appropriate for the group. To maintain momentum for the interest and ideas that are created in the workshop, it is important to agree on some immediate action and a follow-up event. The immediate action could be to email a colleague and share a highlight of the workshop or to act on one item from a list of ideas that comes out of the workshop, or some other next steps participants agree to.

Facilitating at Your Best

The facilitator's role in Appreciative Inquiry is to be a catalyst for change that works in the affirmative, continually guiding organizational members to discover what energizes them, what is possible to produce, what inspires them, and what fills them with hope and possibility. Furthermore, you model the way to openly share knowledge, resources, and learning and you are transparent with your process so participants can make it their own.

As a start, here is an invitation to reflect appreciatively on your own strengths as a facilitator. Think back over your facilitation experiences to date. Recall a time when you have facilitated at your best. You might like to do this with another member of your team or on your own. Do what serves you best.

Discovery Interview

As you think about your experiences as a facilitator, offering your facilitation expertise to groups and helping them clarify their needs, strengths, goals, priorities, aspirations, and results, remember a time when you felt at your best as a facilitator. What was happening? Who was there? What were you doing? What were the participants doing? What are you most proud of? In your high-point story, what are the things you valued most about:

- Yourself and the strengths and qualities of your facilitation?
- The intention and nature of your work?
- Its organization (how it was organized)?

Dream — Future Possibility

You fall into a deep sleep and wake up … and it's two years later. Through your workshop design and facilitation practice, your participants have grown personally and professionally, and your organization has changed in the ways you had imagined; for example, it could be that the number of customers has doubled; finances are extra healthy; the workforce is growing with new candidates wanting to join the organization; investments have been made in sustainable products and refurbishings; and there is a childcare facility. Leadership has congratulated you for your contribution to the success of the business and you have added two new members to your own team.

1. What do *you* dream for your work as a facilitator? What are your positive imaginings of a future that would fulfill you personally and professionally? Describe what you see yourself doing in two years' time in prose, in verse, as a picture—whatever comes most naturally to you.

2. Which elements of the appreciative worldview, including positivity and strength-based approaches, have you integrated most naturally into your work?

3. Which aspect of your work gives you a heightened sense of engagement and meaning?

4. Having grown in these two years, what now are your highest aspirations to further your reach and connection with others?

5. Which Appreciative Inquiry principles or practices are you continuing to strengthen in your practice? How will they continue to expand your dream?

General Guidelines for All Workshops

In keeping with the principles, process, and practice of Appreciative Inquiry, each workshop follows a format and a flow, as described earlier in this section. Below are delivery tips and guidelines to help you create high-energy workshops and to ensure your participants produce work they will be proud of. Some of the following suggestions may seem basic and obvious. I feel they are worth including, as you will have a sense of how to introduce the workshops. Moreover, if you are just starting off in this field, I trust you will find the tips useful. You, as facilitator, knowing you have added value to your participants and your organization, will also feel positively energized.

- The workshop title describes the end state—that which you are working to create.

- Prior to the workshop, read through the entire workshop to make sure the content is as relevant for your participants as possible.

- Make sure you have read and understood the material in Part II of this book so that you are able to talk about Appreciative Inquiry as a change method when you think that will add some benefit to the group's learning and/or can explain terminology such as "positive core."

- Note the suggested times for each focus area and make adjustments to times if necessary, ensuring you allow adequate time to finish without rushing.

- Ensure you have materials for the Dream phase (usually Focus 3) if you intend to make it creative, fun, and playful (recommended).

- Decide what other tools or props will make the workshop more potent, such as music, photographs, inspiring quotes, fruit, water, sweets, flowers, or books in the room. You want to make the environment as inviting as you can to create an ambiance of creativity and to signal a new way of working together.

- Welcome your participants to the workshop in your authentic manner, covering the following points:

  We're going to spend the next _____ hours on the topic of

  _____.

  Our workshop format is totally experiential. You will begin by interviewing each other in pairs and small groups and, from time to time, I will invite you all back together so we can update each other about our discoveries and what else we are learning about our topic of _____.

  Each of you has a worksheet you will work through, starting off in pairs. It would be great if you paired up with someone you know least well.

  My role as facilitator is to guide the process by acting as a host.

  You all have experience, knowledge, skills, ideas, ideals, aspirations, and recommendations to offer related to the topic. That's a purpose of this workshop: to gather the collective knowledge and together create new knowledge, make sense of it, and go out and apply it wisely.

  Here's the process. If at any stage something is unclear, please ask.

  Write your name on your worksheet.

  Select your interview partner (someone you now have the opportunity to learn more about).

  Whoever is the first interviewer reads out loud the "Lead-In Statement."

  Next the interviewers read the first question, using the bullet points as prompts, as necessary, and the interviewees tell stories that describe a high-peak experience associated with the topic.

  The interviewers take a few notes—nothing too detailed—on the interviewees' worksheets (so they have the notes to refer to later).

  The questions and the bullet points are guides and prompts. If curiosity takes you elsewhere, but still on topic, follow it.

  The single most important aspect of the interview is the mindset with which you enter into this workshop. That mindset is one of curiosity. You are having a conversation. It's not an interrogation!

  Stay open to curiosity; remember you are listening to your colleague's story, so it is his or her truth you have the privilege to be listening to.

In twenty to thirty minutes, I will ask you to change roles so that the interviewers now become the interviewees and you start again from reading the "Lead-In Statement" and follow the prompts, leading with your genuine curiosity about your interview partner's peak experience related to this topic.

- After forty to sixty minutes (or the time allocated to complete both interviews), the interview pairs link up with other pairs to form clusters of four to six people.

- Step into facilitation mode and ask them in their new groups of four to six to share the highlights of the stories and to pull our common themes and identify one story that best exemplifies most, if not all of, the themes (Focus 2).

- As facilitator, invite each group to tell its one exemplary story.

- Then ask them to call out the common strengths and themes across all stories that lead to the identifying the "positive core."

- The positive core becomes the data from which the Dream and the Design steps are created (Focuses 3 and 4).

- From this point on, they continue to work in small groups. From time to time, a workshop calls for some personal reflection.

- Facilitate a final debriefing and establish what's happening next.

- Remember that the timing charts for each workshop are guides only.

Summary of Process

The twenty-one highly interactive workshops that follow are designed to get the room buzzing with conversation as pairs embark on their first interviews, then link up with others to form small groups to share best stories of high-point experiences from which common themes begin to emerge. Once you unleash the energy of the participants, it's hard to stop the momentum. The discovery interview of high-point experiences is the initial step of inquiry and begins to shift the levels of energy, setting in motion the potential to embrace change, create new mindsets, and reveal emotions and behaviors in a generative way. From the very first question asked, there is the potential for transformational change and to begin the shift toward living and working with greater consciousness and building strength-based organizations.

Creating Change Positively

Timing and Process — 3 hours, 40 minutes	Benefits and Outcomes
Focus 1 — 40 minutes • 20 minutes for each interview **Focus 2 — 70 minutes** • 30 minutes for groups to share stories • 15 minutes to debrief and facilitate the positive core after Q4 • 15 minutes for groups to respond to Q5 and you facilitate their collective responses • 10 minutes for groups to respond to Q6 **Focus 3 — 55 minutes** • 30 minutes to create the dream • 15 minutes to present and discuss • 10 minutes facilitated debriefing **Focus 4 — 45 minutes** • 15 minutes in groups • 10 minutes facilitated debriefing • 10 minutes personal reflection • 10 minutes facilitated debriefing **Buffer time — 10 minutes for short break and allow additional time for activities and longer debriefings.**	You might select this workshop if change is occurring and there is some resistance or discomfort in the organization. The optimal timing of this workshop would be that you know changes are planned and you invite members to attend this workshop to help them prepare for the changes. In this workshop, participants focus on the high points of a previous change experience. Discovering what worked in the past, they envision how they can position themselves to embrace change in a more positive and expansive way in the future. Identifying what worked, they plan what they can do personally, a project that the team may be undertaking, and how leadership can be supportive during times of change.

Creating Change Positively Worksheet

Lead-In Statement

Mention "change" and, in most cases, it provokes feelings of concern, resistance, and anxiety. Change has high points and low points. For now, let's focus on the high points of a previous change experience. Think of a time when you experienced change and it was a positive experience. It may not have started that way, but it ended up positive for you. Discovering what worked in the past reminds us all that we can change successfully. Building on those capacities, envision how you can position yourself to embrace change in a more positive and expansive way in the future. Identifying what works, imagine what you can do personally on the next change initiative, or plan a project that the team can undertake and recommend how leadership can be supportive during times of change.

Focus 1 — Discover High Points in a Positive Change Story

Paired Interviews

1. Thinking back on previous change experiences, there will have been high points and low points. Let's focus on the high points of a change experience, when it all worked out well in the end.

   - Tell your story.
   - Describe what was happening.
   - Who was involved?
   - What were you doing?

2. Without being humble, what were some of the specific things about you that made the change positive?

   - What are some things you did, thought, and felt? What are you proud of?

"Instead of instilling fear, if a company offered a way for everyone in the business to dive within—to start expanding energy and intelligence—people would work overtime for free. They would be far more creative. And the company would just leap forward. This is the way it can be. It's not the way it is, but it could be that way so easily."

David Lynch (b. 1946)

3. What were some of the helpful contributions of others, for example:

- Ways the change was planned, organized, and communicated;
- How leadership contributed;
- The way relationships helped; and
- The timing of it all.

Focus 2 — Three Wishes to Help Create Change Positively

Interview Pairs Combine to Form Groups of Four or Six

4. In your small groups, interviewers introduce their interview partners and share the high points of their partners' stories of "Creating Change Positively."

- As you listen respectfully, focus on the common themes that come up in the stories.
- Select one story that exemplifies the strengths and successes in creating change positively to present to other groups. These attributes represent the "positive core" in creating change positively.

5. From the collective stories you've heard about creating change positively, what themes emerge: themes of strengths, assets, success factors?

6. Building on your high points, if you could grant three wishes to make the next change a positive experience, what would those wishes be for

- You and your colleagues?
- Leadership?
- The organization?

"I embrace emerging experience. I participate in discovery. I am a butterfly. I am not a butterfly collector, I want the experience of a butterfly."
William Stafford (1914–1993)

Focus 3—Dream, Envisioning the Best Possible Pathway to Change

Small Groups

7. You are now preparing for another change initiative. Building on your positive change stories and wishes, what's the best possible change you can envision?

   - What are the things you value and want to keep or continue doing?

   - What new things would you create to ensure the change will succeed, e.g., new policies, procedures, structures, tools, technology, products, communication strategies?

   - What things will help you navigate through complex transitions from the old to the new more successfully?

   - Present your group's *dream* as creatively as you wish; for example, draw a picture, make a collage, perform a skit, sing a song, or write a poem or a news release.

Focus 4—Feedback and Feedforward

Small Groups and Individual Reflection

8. What's a project your team can take on to strengthen your "change muscle"?

   - What would you do if you were in charge?

   - How would you communicate and inform your staff about changes?

9. Focusing on the positive aspects of change, what has been a high point for you today?

   - What's one small thing you will do after you leave this workshop that will help you focus on the positive aspects of change?

   - What encouragement and support would you give to colleagues who are embarking on change?

> "The greatest good you can do for another is not just share your riches, but reveal to their own."
> Benjamin Disraeli
> (1804–1881)

> "Emus and kangaroos feature on the Australian coat of arms because neither creature can walk backwards."
> Anonymous

Shared Leadership

Timing and Process—2 hours, 35 minutes	Benefits and Outcomes
Focus 1—60 minutes • 30 minutes for each interview **Focus 2—65 minutes** • 30 minutes for groups to share stories • 20 minutes to facilitate the positive core after Q7 • 15 minutes, including facilitated debriefing of Q8 **Focus 3—30 minutes** • 15 minutes Q9 • 5 minutes Q10 • 10 minutes facilitated debriefing	You might select this workshop when there is confusion around roles and accountability. This often occurs when people take on different roles and accountabilities as members of different project teams. In this workshop, participants explore the conditions that allow for shared leadership and how responsibility and accountability are clearly attached to the roles they take on. Through the process, they come to realize how they can assert their leadership at different times, and that not speaking up can be a disservice to everyone. Participants leave with a sense of their own leadership potential and what they can develop.

Shared Leadership Worksheet

Lead-In Statement

We have all been in leadership roles at various times in our lives—not necessarily formal leadership, but still we have taken the lead in some way. When, why, and how we do that depends on a number of factors: what the situation calls for; our ability and willingness to do so; our experience, knowledge and skill sets for the task at hand; as well as our personalities and beliefs about the need for and role of leadership at the time. We assume leadership in our families, our recreational pursuits, and in our workplaces as we move in and out of different situations and projects. In this inquiry about you and leadership, recall an experience about sharing leadership in some way. Let's explore the conditions that allow for shared leadership and how responsibility and accountability are clearly attached to the role of leadership. Moreover, a key component of leadership is to develop leadership in others, so what is your experience of encouraging the leader to come out in all of us?

Focus 1 — Shared Leadership

Paired Interviews

1. Recall a time when you experienced shared leadership at work, at play, or in a relationship.

   - Tell your story.
   - What was it about?
   - What made it shared leadership?
   - Describe what was happening.
   - Who was involved?

2. What do you value about your role in this story?

   - What did you do specifically?
   - What were your strengths?
   - How did you feel?

> "To lead the people, walk behind them."
> Lao-Tzu (600 B.C.)

3. What do you value about the other people involved?

   - Who were they?

   - How were their behaviors supportive to sharing leadership?

4. What do you value about how the set-up for shared leadership was organized? For example:

   - What resources were available?

   - What was the overall environment like?

   - What else supported shared leadership?

5. What observations or comments can you make about responsibility and accountability in your story?

6. How do you demonstrate your leadership?

   - What three wishes do you have about your own leadership qualities?

Focus 2—The Value of Leadership

Interview Pairs Combine to Form Groups of Four or Six

7. In your small groups, interviewers introduce their interview partners and share highlights of their partners' stories of "Shared Leadership."

   - As you listen respectfully, focus on the common themes that come up in the stories.

   - Select one story that exemplifies the positive attributes of shared leadership. These positive attributes represent the "positive core"—the assets and the environment that shared leadership thrives on.

8. What do you most value and appreciate about leadership in your current environment or workplace?

   - Which aspects of leadership can be shared, and what would be the benefits of sharing those aspects?

> "To get others to come along into our ways of thinking, we must go over to theirs; and it is necessary to follow, in order to lead."
>
> William Hazlitt (1738–1830)

> "Leadership and learning are indispensable to each other."
> John F. Kennedy
> (1917–1963)

Focus 3—Let's Do It!

Small Groups and Individual Reflection

9. When we feel good about what we do, everything seems easier; we feel more expansive and generous. We put aside our egos and personal agendas and just do it. If we focus on what we can do, with our best intentions, it just happens. What will you do to bring out leadership in others?

10. What new insights have you had today about shared leadership?

Appreciating Collaborations

Timing and Process—3 hours, 20 minutes	Benefits and Outcomes
Focus 1—50 minutes • 25 minutes for each interview **Focus 2—60 minutes** • 30 minutes for groups to share stories • 20 minutes for groups to respond to Q5 • 10 minutes to debrief responses and chart the positive core **Focus 3—60 minutes** • 30 minutes to create the dream • 15 minutes to present • 15 minutes facilitated debriefing **Focus 4—25 minutes** • 10 minutes personal reflection and conversation • 15 minutes facilitated debriefing to process learnings and takeaways **Buffer time—5 minutes for short break and allow additional time for activities and longer debriefings.**	This workshop is especially helpful for diverse groups to come together. They may not be co-located; they will have their own interests to protect, as well as much to share, and will most likely come from different cultural backgrounds. The goal of the workshop is for participants to hear each other's experiences of former collaborations and take the best to incorporate into future collaborations, thus positioning themselves to embrace collaboration in a more positive and expansive way in the future.

Appreciating Collaborations Worksheet

Lead-In Statement

Collaboration refers to people coming together to produce something they all contribute to in a variety of ways. Increasingly, in our burgeoning global, knowledge economy, with virtual teams spread across the world representing different cultures, the need for productive collaboration is a topic of enormous interest. We have technologies to help us access more information, generate our own content on blogs, and participate on others' blogs, wikis, social networking spaces, and so on. This way of working in cyberspace is location-neutral. We could be sitting in a cubicle across the room, or across the world in a different time zone. It is very exciting to have such a rich diversity of minds and emotions working on projects together. The values of trust, respect, and appreciation for difference are still required—and possibly even more so in virtual environments. Furthermore, it is important to recognize that the "right" way or the "only" way isn't the domain of one group anymore. It helps if we are open and flexible to outcomes that are unknown and unpredictable and hold the belief that we are all doing the best we can with the resources we have.

Focus 1—Best Collaborative Experiences

Paired Interviews

1. What's been the most successful collaboration you have been involved in? What did you appreciate about the whole situation?

   - In your story, describe some of the qualities or practices that made the collaboration in your story successful, for example: purpose, vision, roles, goals, responsibilities, people's attitudes, communication, tools, and so on.

> "Never doubt that a small group of thoughtful, committed citizens can change the world; indeed, it's the only thing that ever has."
> Margaret Mead
> (1901–1978)

2. What did you value about your own contribution to this collaboration?

- What and how did you contribute?
- What motivated you?
- How did you feel?

3. What did you value about the other collaborators?

- What and how did they contribute?
- How did both similarities and differences help the overall experience?

Focus 2—Most Compelling Realizations

Interview Pairs Combine to Form Groups of Four or Six

4. In your small groups, interviewers share highlights of their partners' stories of "appreciating collaborations."

- As you listen respectfully, focus on the common themes that come up in the stories.
- Select a story that you agree reflects all or most of the common themes and share it with the other groups.

5. Of all the stories you've heard, what are the best or most successful attributes of collaborating—its "positive core"—those factors that make collaborations vibrant, energizing, and satisfying.

Focus 3—Creating a Template for a New Collaboration

Small Groups

6. Imagine that next month you are presenting to a group of participants who are undertaking a corporate social responsibility initiative. Your team recommends the sponsors approach

"Man's mind stretched to a new idea never goes back to its original dimensions."
Oliver Wendell Holmes
(1809–1894)

the project as true collaboration among cross-sector multi-stakeholder groups so that all perspectives are considered and diverse resources and expertise will be available.

- What are the most compelling reasons you'd give to encourage them to approach this initiative as collaboration versus approaching it as discrete individuals, intact teams, or homogeneous groups—such as only IT, only strategy, only marketing, only engineering, only government, only one demographic, etc?

- How might you help them envision other possible benefits and positive outcomes of collaboration?

- Present your group's template for collaboration as creatively as you wish to the other groups. It could be a drawing, a collage, a performance, a song, a poem. Be imaginative and enjoy it!

Focus 4—Reflection and Anticipation

Groups and Individual Reflection

7. Having told and heard stories about successful collaborations of the past and imagined future possibilities, what new insights and learnings have you gained today?

8. Looking to your next collaboration, what will you most look forward to contributing and paying attention to?

"We will either find a way, or make one."
Hannibal (247–182 B.C.)

Valuing Technology

Timing and Process — 2 hours, 45 minutes	Benefits and Outcomes
Focus 1 — 40 minutes • 20 minutes for each interview **Focus 2 — 40 minutes** • 30 minutes for groups to share stories and report out the exemplary story • 10 minutes to facilitate the positive core after Q4 **Focus 3 — 50 minutes** • 30 minutes to create the dream • 10 minutes to present • 10 minutes facilitated debriefing **Focus 4 — 30 minutes** • 15 minutes in groups for Q7 and Q8 • 5 minutes for individual reflection • 10 minutes facilitated debriefing **Buffer time — 5 minutes for short break and allow additional time for activities and longer debriefings.**	You might select this workshop because, with ever-changing technology, systems, and software, people feel often overburdened with having to continually learn new processes and systems. In this workshop, participants share their knowledge of the most exciting technology in any field that serves humanity and then, more particularly, the technology that serves them in their own workplaces. They also envision what else is possible in their immediate environments and make recommendations for enhancements to the systems they use today so that it will serve them and their clients better in the future.

Valuing Technology Worksheet

Lead-In Statement

Technology has been supporting us since 50,000 years ago when our hunter-gatherer ancestors constructed the club to enhance their livelihoods. Applying the knowledge of what that tool could do for them helped them survive, which was a wise thing to do. We define wisdom as the practical (and moral) application of knowledge. Today, in the twenty-first century, we have so much more knowledge. The big question is: Are we applying it wisely? Our tools and technologies continue to meet and even surpass the emerging needs of our changing social landscape. It's hard to imagine how, in every part of the world today, we would function without emerging technology. Technology serves to make routine work and processes easier and faster, freeing people up to do more creative and complex work. Once we learn how to use and apply newer technologies, our lives can be made so much easier at work and home. Already, so many outstanding technologies are adding value to our lives. The potential for improved performance and enhanced quality of products and lifestyle is without boundaries.

Focus 1 — Best Contributions of Technology

Paired Interviews

1. What is the most innovative technology you are aware of today, in any field—art, health, education, transportation, manufacturing?

   - Describe in detail some of the innovative technologies you know about and what they do.

     - What are their benefits to the customers they serve?

     - What excites your about these technologies?

"Any sufficiently advanced technology is indistinguishable from magic."

Arthur C. Clarke
(1917–2008)

2. What technologies do you use in your current job?

   - How do they serve you and your clients and customers?

   - How is your work and the quality of your work and life helped by these technologies?

Focus 2 — Technology That Serves

Interview Pairs Combine to Form Groups of Four or Six

3. In your small groups, the interviewers introduce their partners and share highlights of their partners' two stories: (1) best technology they are aware of and (2) how they are best using technology at work.

   - What common themes reveal the best and most successful experiences with technology?

   - Select one story from your small group that illustrates impressive technology and share it with the other groups.

4. Generate a list of best attributes of how technologies are helping humankind in all walks of life—health, education, environment, entertainment, transportation, manufacturing, and so on.

Focus 3 — Future Possibilities

Small Groups

5. Imagine that it's five years into the future and you come to work and you have the best and most helpful technology for your job. What types of technology are you using, and what do they allow you and others to do or experience differently?

6. Be as creative as you can in imagining your future workplace. Show how you really enjoy your new technologies and equipment—you get great benefits, your friends and kids think it's awesome. What else would be a terrific asset

> "It is the framework which changes with each new technology and not just the picture within the frame."
> Marshall McLuhan
> (1911–1980)

of technology to make your job satisfying, enjoyable, and meaningful?

- Present your future technology-enhanced workplace to the other groups in a creative way: a drawing, a skit, a metaphor, a media format, whatever way will help you put your dream technologies across.

- In your imaged future, how have you been trained and how are you keeping up-to-date to ensure you are continually at the leading edge of technological innovations?

Focus 4—Immediate Enhancements

Small Group and Individual Reflection

7. Based on your current experiences and what you imagine is possible, what enhancements do you recommend right now that will add to the quality of your work life and the experience of colleagues and customers?

8. In order to make sure that the technology in your workplace is the most helpful it can possibly be, what could be implemented in the next year or so? What would it take to implement?

9. What beginning steps could you recommend, and what might be some short-term beneficial impacts?

"The science of today is the technology of tomorrow."
Edward Teller (1908–2003)

Unleashing Creativity for Continuous Innovation

Timing and Process—3 hours, 25 minutes	Benefits and Outcomes
Focus 1—50 minutes • 25 minutes for each interview **Focus 2—60 minutes** • 30 minutes for groups to share stories and identify themes, including your facilitation of the positive core after Q3 • 30 minutes for responses to Q4, including your debriefing the groups' responses **Focus 3—50 minutes** • 30 minutes to create the dream • 10 minutes to present • 10 minutes facilitated debriefing **Focus 4—30 minutes** • 10 minutes to facilitate responses to Q7 • 10 minutes personal reflection to Q8 and Q9 • 10 minutes facilitated debriefing **Buffer time—15 minutes for short break and to allow additional time for activities and longer debriefing.**	You might select this workshop because you know people are a little timid at stretching themselves. In this workshop, participants recall times when they were creative and they work through what it takes to bring their creative beings to the workplace. They identify the conditions they need in order to optimize their productivity and performance in a creative way. They apply their insights with a creative presentation of how unleashing innate creativity will impact their work.

Unleashing Creativity for Continuous Innovation Worksheet

Lead-In Statement

We have the capacity to be creative, even though many of us will deny that we are naturally creative. We tend to limit our thinking about creativity by placing it in the artistic domains of painting, music, theater, writing, or film or we think it belongs to some jobs and not others, for example, advertising, public relations, gaming, and so forth. In the workplace, there are endless opportunities to exercise creativity, even though we may think our creative capacity is thwarted. It doesn't have to be this way. There will have been times, at work or at play, when you were fully absorbed in an activity and you could say you were firing on all cylinders. It may have been easy or it may have been challenging—and it may have been both. Nevertheless, you were creative. It could be that you came up with a different or new way of presenting an idea or a spreadsheet or a policy change. What does it takes to bring your full creative being to the workplace, and what are the conditions you need to optimize your productivity and performance using your creative ideas? Moreover, what is your responsibility for speaking up about all your talents and ideas you are passionate about?

Focus 1—Conditions for Creativity

Paired Interviews

1. In the past when you produced something new, it is likely you accessed something of your "creative juices" or you were on a roll.

   - What did you create (a piece of music, a presentation, a skit, a meeting agenda, a video, a piece of jewelry, a blog, a product)?

> "There are two ways of being creative. One can sing and dance. Or one can create an environment in which singers and dancers flourish."
> Warren G. Bennis (b. 1925)

- What was that experience like?

- What facilitated your creativity? Was it your skill sets, knowledge, resources, attitude, belief, desire, encouragement from others?

- Who else was there, and what was it like?

- Tell the story.

2. What were the most significant conditions that supported your creative expression?

   - Think back to what helped you. What were your mindset, tools, people, time, passion, and expectations?

Focus 2—Productivity and Creative Energy

Interview Pairs Combine to Form Groups of Four or Six

3. In your small groups, interviewers introduce their partners and share the highlights of their stories about a time when they were creative.

   - Listen for the common themes that came up to reveal talents, strengths, assets, and the conditions that lead to success on unleashing creativity.

   - What is your collective "positive core"?

4. At work, how are you expressing your creativity? What examples can you give?

   - What percentage of your time and effort is currently spent in exercising your own creativity?

   - What do these examples and percentages say about how creativity and innovation are valued in your workplace?

   - What realistically can you do or are you willing to do to be more creative in your work? What positive impact will that have on you, your work, and others?

> "Never before in history has innovation offered promise of so much to so many in so short a time."
>
> Bill Gates (b. 1955)

- How will you let colleagues and your boss know that you'd like to have more opportunities to show greater creativity?

Focus 3 — Unleashing Your Creativity

Group Work

5. Imagine your workplace is the most innovative of its kind. What would that be like from your perspective?

    - Is it about people's skills, intelligence, experience, talents, temperament, goodwill, networks, leadership, recognition, and rewards?

    - Is it about technologies?

    - It is about culture?

    - Is it about policy, regulation, and governance?

6. In a creative way, present your group's imagined most innovative workplace, incorporating the factors that you think are most important. It could be a performance, a collage, a picture, a story, a media story of some kind. Use your imaginations creatively.

Focus 4 — Climate for Creativity

Group Work and Individual Reflection

7. What are the strengths of the organization that facilitate creativity and innovation?

8. How do you want to lend your creativity to foster innovation?

9. What positive changes will you make so you can maximize your creativity?

> "It is better to create than to be learned; creating is the true essence of life."
> Barthold Georg Niebuhr
> (1776–1831)

High-Performing Teams

Timing and Process—3 hours, 10 minutes	Benefits and Outcomes
Focus 1—40 minutes • 20 minutes for each interview **Focus 2—60 minutes** • 30 minutes for groups to share stories and report out the exemplary story from each group. • 30 minutes to facilitate the positive core and three wishes after Q4 **Focus 3—55 minutes** • 30 minutes to create the dream • 10 minutes to present • 15 minutes facilitated debriefing after Q8 **Focus 4—25 minutes** • 10 minutes for personal reflection • 15 minutes facilitated debriefing **Buffer time—10 minutes for short break and to allow additional time for activities and longer debriefings.**	You might select this workshop because it is important to clarify roles and responsibilities as members move in and out of different project teams. In this workshop, participants will share their experiences of working in a successful team. Once they identify the strengths of their own contributions and the contributions of others, together they co-create ways forward, building on their existing strengths to design ways they can further strengthen the existing team.

High-Performing Teams Worksheet

Lead-In Statement

Teams, teamwork, and team building are important topics. We work in teams to bring the best people and resources to a situation. We come with different skill sets, personalities, and motivations, so it's always dynamic. Effectiveness is enhanced when people have goal clarity, role clarity, a clear leadership process, and clearly articulated responsibilities. Yet, with the valuable diversity we have in our communities, we know that personality preferences, thinking styles, social interactions, belief systems, and values impact how we relate. So what is it that makes a truly high-performing team? We have all been part of a high-performing team at some point, even a team of two! Let's access those high-point experiences of good team performance. Let's identify the strengths of our contributions and the contributions of others and, together, we can co-create ways forward, building on our existing strengths—our positive core—to design ways we can further strengthen the existing team.

Focus 1—Stories of High-Performing Teams

Paired Interviews

1. Recall a story of a time when you were a member of a team that was performing really well—it was a most successful team.

   - What made it a high-performing team?
   - What about roles, goals, leadership, communications, behaviors, and the impact those factors had on the team?
   - What else impacted the team positively?

2. In remembering your story:

   - What was your role in the team and the strengths you brought to it?

> "Individually, we are one drop. Together, we are an ocean."
>
> Ryunosuke Satoro

- What were the individual strengths of team members?
- How did they also contribute to the success of the team?
- How would you describe the team spirit?
- What were some of the feelings expressed about the experience?

Focus 2 — Further Strengthening Our Team

Interview Pairs Combine to Form Groups of Four or Six

3. In your small groups, interviewers share highlights of their interview partners' stories of most successful team experiences.

   - As you listen respectfully, focus on the common themes that reveal the collective strengths of the teams.
   - Select one story that exemplifies the strengths of successful teams because it that story you will find the "positive core"—those successful attributes of a high-performing team.

4. From the themes you have come up with for your best stories of teamwork, what are your three wishes to further strengthen team performance? For example, it could be related to people, training, finance, environment, technology, strategy, marketing, politics, processes, policies, or something else.

Focus 3 — Dream Team

Small Creative Group Work

5. Taking the existing strengths and capacities of high-performing teams, imagine you come to work tomorrow and you begin to incorporate all those elements to create the best and strongest team you can wish for. What would that team be like?

"We don't accomplish anything in this world alone ... and whatever happens is the result of the whole tapestry of one's life and all the weavings of individual threads from one to another that creates something."
Sandra Day O'Connor
(b. 1930)

6. Use your fullest imagination to describe the work:

   - How you are doing it;
   - The communications;
   - The conversations;
   - How you acknowledge each other's contributions;
   - How you express feelings;
   - How you celebrate;
   - How you take time out;
   - How you learn; and
   - Whatever else you can possibly imagine that will make it a great team.

7. Present your group's dream team as creatively as you wish to the other groups. It could be a drawing, a collage, a performance, a song, a poem. Be imaginative and perform well!

8. What project would you be interested in participating in to strengthen the team? What are some beginning steps you can take?

   - If you were leading this team, what would you do?

Focus 4—Design and Destiny

Individual Reflection and Facilitated Debriefing

9. What has been a highlight of this session?

10. What do you value about your contribution today?

11. What do you value about others' contributions today?

12. What do you value about your team?

"Team spirit is what gives so many companies an edge over their competitors."
George L. Clements

Compassionate Connections

Timing and Process—3 hours	Benefits and Outcomes
Focus 1—40 minutes • 20 minutes for each interview **Focus 2—45 minutes** • 35 minutes for groups to share stories and report out one exemplary story • 10 minutes to facilitate the positive core—the themes of strengths/highest value after Q4 **Focus 3—50 minutes** • 30 minutes to create the dream • 10 minutes to present • 10 minutes facilitated debriefing **Focus 4—35 minutes** • 15 minutes in groups • 10 minutes facilitated debriefing • 5 minutes personal reflection for Q7 and Q8 • 5 minutes facilitated debriefing **Buffer time—10 minutes for short break and to allow additional time for activities and longer debriefings.**	Instead of focusing on negativity, on difference, on self-interest, this workshop invites participants to flip the coin and see a situation from a heartfelt place of common humanity. In this workshop, participants share their stories of experiencing or witnessing compassion. They identify what compassion looks like in our big cities in our day-to-day life as all of us go about earning a living, looking after our families, educating our children. What does compassion look like at work? Participants define what compassion is and why it is important. They leave with a personal commitment of how they can show their compassionate, caring selves.

Compassionate Connections Worksheet

Lead-In Statement

Sometimes it's good to stop, take a deep breath, and reflect on the topic of how we live our lives. What is it that connects us to our fellow human beings and to the whole of nature—the sky, the land, the sea, and all other creatures? What are the universals that remind us simultaneously of our smallness and our grandeur? Individually, we are just specks in the universe, yet our potential and capacity are huge. We can be proud of what we do, and it can also be humbling. Increasingly, we understand that we live in an interconnected world and that we are all interdependent. For us all to flourish, we cannot allow one person to suffer. What does compassion look like in our big cities in our day-to-day lives as we go about earning a living, looking after our families, educating our children? What does compassion look like in countries far removed from life as we know it? What is compassion? Why is it important? How can we show our compassionate, caring selves?

Focus 1—Modeling Compassion

Paired Interviews

1. Remember a time when you experienced a deep connection with others and a sense of compassion filled you—you reacted in a way that strengthened your sense of being in community with others.

   - Describe the situation. What happened?

   - How were you involved—as a participant or as an observer?

   - What about that experience filled you with a sense of compassionate connection to others?

"To care for anyone else enough to make their problems one's own, is ever the beginning of one's real ethical development."
Felix Adler (1851–1933)

- What did you notice at the time about the behavior of others involved?

- What did you notice about yourself in this story of compassionate connection?

- What did you notice about your feelings? Where did you feel those feelings in your body?

Focus 2 — Sustaining Compassion

Interview Pairs Combine to Form Groups of Four or Six

2. In small groups, interviewers share highlights of their interview partners' stories of "compassionate connections."

   - As you listen respectfully, focus on the common themes that reveal the collective attributes of the compassionate experiences.

3. Select one story that exemplifies the qualities of compassion from your group to share with other groups.

4. As you reflect on your story and hear the stories of others, what common themes emerge that speak to what moves us to feel compassion toward other human beings?

Focus 3 — Imagine, All of Us Part of One Another

Group Work

5. In the words of Thomas Merton, author: "The whole idea of compassion is based on a keen awareness of the interdependence of all these living beings, which are all part of one another, and all involved in one another." What if you should wake up and ten years have passed and we are living in ways that show we are all so much more aware of the interdependence of all living beings. What are you seeing in

"I would rather feel compassion than know the meaning of it."
Thomas Aquinas
(1225–1274)

this world where we are "all part of one another"? What is new and inspiring for you?

6. Present your group's dream as creatively as you wish to the other groups. It could be a drawing, a collage, a performance, a song, a poem, showing the value of "compassionate connections"—all being part of one another.

Focus 4—Your Inspiration

Group Work and Individual Reflection

7. Of all the characters—real or fictional—that exemplify compassion, whom do you most connect with? Without necessarily identifying your chosen character, what qualities do you admire that this person has?

- Which aspects of your chosen character are you inspired to further develop in yourself?
- How will you do that?
- What results do you hope for?

8. What have you valued about this session on "compassionate connections"?

"If you want others to be happy, practice compassion. If you want to be happy, practice compassion."
  His Highness the Dalai Lama

Strength-Based Coaching

Timing and Process—3 hours, 15 minutes	Benefits and Outcomes
Focus 1—40 minutes • 20 minutes for each interview **Focus 2—60 minutes** • 20 minutes for groups to share stories • 30 minutes to prepare responses to Q6 and for group to share personal statements • 10 minutes for facilitated debriefing **Focus 3—50 minutes** • 40 minutes for both coaching sessions (20 minutes × 2) • 10 minutes for facilitated debriefing **Focus 4—30 minutes** • 15 minutes for personal reflection and coaching plan • 15 minutes for facilitated debriefing **Buffer time—15 minutes for short break and to allow additional time for activities and longer debriefings.**	If creating a coaching culture is a goal, this workshop will be a good start. In this workshop, participants experience a coaching model that starts with what is working well and facilitates conversation around their natural strengths, talents, and preferences. They learn there are choice points. They can pay attention to the weaknesses in a situation, or the strengths, and they can determine what has greater leverage. From a strength-based perspective, they identify their attributes and positive contributions and the attributes and positive contributions of colleagues. In this workshop, participants experience coaching from a strength-based perspective.

Strength-Based Coaching Worksheet
Lead-In Statement

Coaching is about improvement, going to the next level, achieving aspirations, identifying ways to live to one's fullest capacity and potential. A dominant traditional model of coaching has been to find out what's wrong in order to eliminate weaknesses, fix the "problem," and even draw attention to past failures. Strengths-based coaching comes from the worldview that in every system (human and otherwise) there are also many things that already work right. Our coaching model starts with what is working well—our natural strengths, talents, and preferences. We recognize there are choice points. We focus on what consumes us. Said another way: "Where the attention goes, the energy flows." As leaders, colleagues, parents, and educators, is it not our responsibility to encourage the development of others in life—nurturing ways to help them live in the fullest and most satisfying ways possible and strengthen their existing talents? Pertinent to the concept of strengths-based coaching is David Cooperrider's reference to a conversation he had with the late management guru, Peter Drucker, who said: "The task of leadership is to create an alignment of strengths, making our weaknesses irrelevant."

Focus 1—Introduction to Identifying Strengths

Paired Interview

"When I dare to be powerful, to use my strength in the service of my vision, then it becomes less and less important whether I am afraid."
Andre de Lorde (1871–1933)

1. We go through highs and lows in all aspects of our lives. Thinking back on the last six to twelve months, reflect on a "high-point" moment—a time that is memorable and stands out when you felt most engaged or challenged, or gained an important insight about your strengths or talents.

    • Please share the story.

    • What was the situation?

- Who else was involved?

- What were you doing?

- What happened that made you more aware of your strengths?

- How did it make you feel?

2. Let's imagine we have a conversation with three people who know you well and asked them to share the three best qualities they see in you. What do you imagine they would say?

3. What's the evidence that they would mention those specific best qualities?

4. From your story and the qualities others have identified as your strengths, what are you conscious of when you are working to your strengths?

- Mentally?

- Emotionally?

- Spiritually?

- Physically?

Focus 2—Acknowledging Your Strengths

Interview Pairs Combine to Form Groups of Four or Six

5. In your small groups, interviewers share highlights of their interview partners' stories of personal strengths

- As you listen respectfully, focus on the common themes related to identifying strengths.

6. What does that say about the talent in this group? Take all your collective experiences and produce an individual statement that captures the essence of what working to your strengths does for you individually and how it feels.

- Read your statements to each other and share insights.

"Every time you don't follow your inner guidance, you feel a loss of energy, loss of power, a sense of spiritual deadness."

Shakti Gawain

Focus 3—Coaching to Strengths

Paired Coaching—Take Turns Coaching Each Other, with the Following Prompts/Questions

7. Choose one of your strengths and remember a time when you lived up to that strength. What happened? How did working to that strength impact your perception of time, productivity, and work satisfaction?

8. As you continuously seek to develop yourself, how will you generate your own inspiration?

   - Which strengths will you develop further?

   - How will you amplify your existing strengths?

   - What possibilities can you imagine when you amplify your strengths?

   - What excites you about this type of coaching?

Focus 4—Developing Your Strength as a Coach

Individual Reflection and Group Debriefing

9. If an objective of strength-based coaching is to support and develop yourself alongside your colleagues, what will you focus on and what can you do to assist others to identify and work to their strengths?

   - How will you use your strengths to develop others?

   - Select a colleague, team, or family member. Identify a number of that person's strengths. Determine what you will say and do to make the person aware of his or her strengths and encourage him or her to further develop those strengths.

> "The deepest craving of human nature is the need to be appreciated."
>
> William James
> (1842–1910)

Respectful Relationships

Timing and Process—2 hours, 30 minutes	Benefits and Outcomes
Focus 1—30 minutes • 15 minutes for each interview **Focus 2—35 minutes** • 30 minutes for groups to share stories and identify common themes or shared strengths across the stories • 5 minutes to facilitate the "positive core" after Q2 **Focus 3—45 minutes** • 30 minutes to integrate (dream) • 10 minutes to present groups' dreams • 5 minutes to debrief **Focus 4—30 minutes** • 10 minutes facilitated debriefing after Q5 • 10 minutes for individual reflection • 10 minutes for a final debriefing **Buffer time—10 minutes for a short break and to allow additional time for activities and longer debriefings.**	You might select this workshop if you need to encourage individuals or diverse groups to appreciate each other's perspectives on the topic of *respect*. In this workshop, participants identify how respect is reflected in behaviors and interactions. They share a range of examples from business situations and look for common themes that cross all sectors. They identify what it takes to make respectful relationships stick and what their own roles are in facilitating respectful relationships.

Respectful Relationships Worksheet

Lead-In Statement

When deep respect is present, the energy between people or the tone in an environment is palpable. We can see it, feel it, and hear it. It touches us. The indicators that respect is a value that is truly lived out are in the behaviors and interactions of individuals. People listen carefully; they are courteous and patient, inquiring and seeking to understand. The pace in our lives has sped up and diversity is enriching our communities. With that, it seems we need to be even more mindful of how we impact others as we rush about. A smile, allowing someone to go ahead of you, showing gratitude for a kindness or acknowledgement, and eye contact when appropriate not only make you feel more generous to others, but it has a domino effect as well. Those to whom we show genuine respect are more likely to exhibit similar respectful behaviors and courtesies to others. What does it take to make respectful relationships contagious? What is our personal role in that?

Focus 1 — Stories of Respectful Relationships

Paired Interviews

"I respect the man who knows distinctly what he wishes. The greater part of all mischief … arises from the fact that men do not sufficiently understand their own aims. They have undertaken to build a tower, and spend no more labor on the foundation than … a hut."

Johann Wolfgang von Goethe (1749–1832)

1. Consider a service or a business encounter you have witnessed or experienced during which you could tell that respect for people was a value not only talked about, but actively lived in this organization.

   - What was your experience of respect about?

   - Describe what was happening.

   - Who was involved?

   - As you recall that story, how did you react? What thoughts, feelings, and actions did you experience?

   - What was memorable about the respectful experience?

2. What were the indicators that respect was highly valued in this business or service organization?

   • Was it the service level, communication style, language, product, courtesy, attention to detail, follow-up, efficiency, respect for their environment?

   • What made the real difference?

Focus 2 — Integration of the Best Examples

Interview Pairs Combine to Form Groups of Four or Six

3. In your small groups, interviewers will introduce their partners and share the highlights of the stories they heard.

   • As you listen respectfully, what are some of common themes or shared strengths that came out of the stories on this topic of Respectful Relationships?

   • Many organizations have "respect" as a core value: respect for employees, customers, or environment, to name a few. What else can you identify from your own stories about "respect" as part of the culture?

Focus 3 — Projecting Your Best Examples Forward

4. Imagine you fall into a deep sleep and, when you awaken, it is a year later and you come into your workplace to find all the best examples of respectful relationships are now being practiced. They are fully integrated into your own team, organization, or business to show an uncompromising respect for people and the environment. What would that look like, sound like, feel like?

   • Create a scenario, a drawing, or a collage or come up with a metaphor or song that shows respectful relationships with all your stakeholders, as well as the environment in which you work.

> "Don't be in a hurry to condemn because he doesn't do what you do or think as you think or as fast. There was a time when you didn't know what you know today."
>
> Malcolm X (1925–1965)

- Enjoy yourselves as you present your creativity to other groups.

Focus 4 — Respecting Your Relationships

Small Groups and Individual Reflection

5. What does it take to sustain respectful relationships? For example, is it up to individuals, management, policies, leading by example?

   - What would you propose? What new elements can you introduce?

   - How would you communicate to others the importance of showing respect? What benefits do you envision?

6. What's been the most valuable thing you've learned or re-learned about respectful relationships as a result of this session?

7. What are you taking away that will strengthen your respect for yourself and for others?

> "To be one, to be united is a great thing. But to respect the right to be different is maybe even greater."
>
> Unknown

Business As a Positive Agent for Change—Leaving a Legacy

Timing and Process—3 hours, 45 minutes	Benefits and Outcomes
Focus 1—60 minutes • 30 minutes for each interview **Focus 2—60 minutes** • 40 minutes for groups to share stories and report out one exemplary story • 20 minutes to facilitate the positive core after Q4 **Focus 3—60 minutes** • 30 minutes to create the dream • 15 minutes to present • 15 minutes Q&A and facilitated debriefing **Focus 4—30 minutes** • 15 minutes for personal reflection • 15 minutes facilitated debriefing **Buffer time—15 minutes for short break and to allow additional time for activities and longer debriefings.**	This workshop can serve a number of audiences for a range of purposes: senior executives or leaders wanting or needing to change direction (for the organization or for themselves, perhaps clarifying a legacy); a group wanting to create a strategy for corporate social responsibility; a group wanting to refocus around a vision and mission. In this workshop, the focus is on clarifying what is important individually and collectively and on identifying the positive changes that already exist and what more is possible.

Business As a Positive Agent for Change — Leaving a Legacy Worksheet

Lead-In Statement

The call of our time is for a new vision that will guide us into the future, a vision based on equity, justice, prosperity, compassion, and the recognition of our interdependence. The role businesses can play is critical and essential. This workshop is based on the global inquiry Business as an Agent of World Benefit (BAWB), spearheaded at the Weatherhead School of Management at Case Western Reserve University in Cleveland, Ohio. BAWB is a search for the organizations that are proactively positioning themselves through their visions and strategies as key players in the world willing to demonstrate that the corporate bottom line and the world's bottom line are not mutually exclusive. Anecdotally, research findings show that good corporate leaders are good community leaders. Employees are far more satisfied at work when they know their work has meaning, that they are doing something good beyond the mundane, and that their work serves a higher purpose. Aligning one's sense of higher purpose with day-to-day living has an energy that not only sustains and is sustainable, but can also lead to flourishing cultures and environments.

Focus 1 — A Larger Sense of Purpose

Paired Interviews

> "The best thing you can do is the right thing. The worst thing you can do is nothing."
> Theodore Roosevelt
> (1858–1919)

1. Thinking about yourself and your work and a larger sense of purpose, what is it that you do now? What most attracted you to your present work—the things you find most meaningful, valuable, satisfying, challenging, or exciting?

   • Tell the story of your journey to this point in your career.

2. A key task in life is to discover and define our life's purpose. Looking back over important times in your life, please share

a story of a time when clarity about life's purpose or your calling emerged for you.

- What was the situation?

- How was your purpose made clear to you?

- How did it make you feel?

- How have you acted on it?

Focus 2 — Sharing Stories

Interview Pairs Combine to Form Groups of Four or Six

3. In your small groups, allow your interview partners to introduce you and share with the others what how you responded to questions 1 and 2 above.

- Now that you have heard highlights of everyone's stories, what common themes about your sense of purpose became clearer?

4. Find one story that seems to illustrate the shared themes and present that story to the other groups.

- How resonant are the themes across the groups, and what are your collective strengths, your existing assets, and your positive core?

Focus 3 — Vision of a Better World

Groups

5. Let's assume that tonight you go into a sound sleep and when you awaken it's ten years into the future and the world has changed in ways you would most like to see.

- What is happening?

- What is new and better?

- How do you know it is better?

"A new vision of development is emerging. Development is becoming a people-centered process, whose ultimate goal must be the improvement of the human condition."

Unknown

- More specifically, how is business a positive agent for change in the world? Describe the ways you see businesses serving and benefiting our world in ten years' time.

- What are their agendas?

- What kind of innovations or opportunities are they creating?

- Knowing there are organizations that are already positive agents for change through practices that nurture the human spirit and metrics that value economic and ecological performance, what else do you see emerging that strengthens existing capabilities to move us in the direction of your vision?

- Prepare a presentation of your visions of a better world in the most creative, inspiring way you want. It could be a media report, a performance, a collage or drawing, a song or poem.

Focus 4—Your Legacy

Individual Reflection and Facilitated Debriefing

"Every great dream begins with a dreamer. Always remember, you have within you the strength, the patience, and the passion to reach for the stars to change the world."

Harriet Tubman
(1820–1913)

6. To translate our visions of the world into reality, it will take each one of us to be mindful of the legacy we pass forward every day. Looking to the future, what might be the next stages in your work, or what do you sense your legacy will be?

7. What is a project you can introduce and champion?

8. What's the smallest step you can take right here, right now?

Nurturing Diversity

Timing and Process—3 hours	Benefits and Outcomes
Focus 1—40 minutes • 20 minutes for each interview **Focus 2—50 minutes** • 30 minutes for groups to share stories and report out the one exemplary story • 5 minutes to facilitate the common themes after Q2 • 15 minutes for groups to respond to Q3, including facilitated debriefing **Focus 3—55 minutes** • 30 minutes to create the dream • 10 minutes to present • 15 minutes facilitated debriefing, including Q7 and Q8 **Focus 4—25 minutes** • 15 minutes of personal reflection and group sharing • 10 minutes facilitated debriefing, including Q11 **Buffer time—10 minutes for a short break and allow additional time for activities and longer debriefings.**	As a result of participating in this workshop, participants will have been made aware of many positives examples of all kinds of diversity and developed a strategy of inclusion. They unpack diversity in all its guises: gender, age, physical, values, thinking, culture, and more. The aim is to shine the light on the value that diversity and inclusion bring into all aspects of our daily lives and come up with ways to nurture it and benefit from it.

Nurturing Diversity Worksheet

Lead-In Statement

"Vive la difference" is an old French saying. "Long live our differences" is perhaps an English equivalent. Imagine the flip side: if everyone in the world were the same, what a boring and scary world it would be! What does it take to truly embrace diversity in its every form? At work, we hear "Diversity is a strategic imperative. It's good for business." What does that mean and how is it lived out? We move beyond prejudice and fear as we learn more about all the different peoples and cultures that make up our world: different languages, body shapes, physical abilities, genders, ages, educational levels, color, talents, and abilities—an extraordinary richness of diversity. Sometimes diversity is more subtle, especially if it is not a physical characteristic, such as diversity of thoughts, beliefs, and value systems, even personality styles. It seems more helpful if we focus on diversity as adding value than if we think about it as separating and dividing us. It's good to be different, just as it's good to be similar. We need both.

Focus 1—Defining Diversity

Paired Interviews

1. What kind of diversity are you aware of as you go about your daily life—gender, cultural, age, and so forth? Tell a story of when you were impacted by an encounter with diversity of some kind and it was a truly positive experience. What are the high points in your story on diversity?

   - What was the occasion?

   - Where were you?

   - Who else was there?

   - How did the diversity factor add value to the situation or the people in a positive way?

"There never were in the world two opinions alike, no more than two hairs or two grains; the most universal quality is diversity."
Michel de Montaigne
(1533–1592)

Focus 2—Diversity and Its Strengths

Interview Pairs Combine to Form Groups of Four or Six

> "Be intrigued by the differences you hear. Expect to be surprised. Treasure curiosity more than certainty.... Remember you don't fear people whose story you know. Real listening always brings people closer together."
>
> Margaret Wheatley (2002), *Turning to One Another*

2. In your small groups, each interviewer should share his or her partner's story of diversity having a positive impact.

   - As you listen respectfully, focus on the common themes that come up in the stories.

   - Select a story that you agree reflects all or most of the common themes and share it with the other groups.

   - Of all the stories you've heard, what are the best or most beneficial outcomes of nurturing diversity? How has it positively impacted situations?

3. What can we do to be more conscious of how diversity is positive force?

Focus 3—Celebrating Our Global Context

In small groups, choose one of the following activities (4 or 5) and present in as creative a way as you can, using all the resources you have—your imagination being the biggest!

4. Imagine you are collaborating with the marketing department of a global rice producer. You are planning next year's advertising campaign. What sort of advertising would you design so that it would resonate with consumers all over the world?

   - How will you incorporate your sensitivities toward valuing diverse groups in the customer base all around the world?

   OR

5. Imagine you are working in collaboration with a team of architects, designing an art gallery to begin construction in a year's time. There is such excitement to create a place of

beauty that includes access for all people, all art forms, and is environmentally state of the art.

- What will you incorporate into your design, your policies, and governance to ensure 100 percent inclusion in all areas?

6. Present your group's imagined project as creatively as you wish to the other groups. It could be a drawing, a collage, a performance, a song, a poem. Be imaginative, have fun, and perform well!

7. How did the presentations impact you?

8. What elements—values, policies, strategies, technologies, and so forth—were common across all presentations? What did some teams include that others did not?

Focus 4—Meanwhile, Back Home ...

Individual Reflection and Group Debriefing

9. What is something you can do to be more conscious of nurturing diversity?

10. What is something you'd recommend your team or organization do to nurture diversity?

11. If you were the boss, what would you do to nurture diversity?

> "We need diversity of thought in the world to face the new challenges."
> Tim Berners-Lee (b. 1955)

Flourishing Communities

Timing and Process—4 hours	Benefits and Outcomes
Focus 1—40 minutes • 20 minutes for each interview **Focus 2—55 minutes** • 30 minutes for groups to share stories • 15 minutes for groups to respond to Q3, including facilitated debriefing • 10 minutes to respond to Q2, including facilitated debriefing **Focus 3—45 minutes** • 30 minutes to create the dream • 10 minutes to present • 5 minutes facilitated debriefing **Focus 4—85 minutes** • Participants self-select into working groups based on the design element they choose • 30 minutes to identify design elements in self-selected teams • 15 minutes to create future possibility statement • 10 minutes facilitated debriefing • 15 minutes in groups for Q10 • 5 minutes of personal reflection • 10 minutes facilitated debriefing **Buffer time—15 minutes for short break and to allow additional time for activities and longer debriefings.**	The aim of this workshop is to invite participants to re-connect with the factors that contribute to a flourishing work group or community of practice. It could be that, of late, some "languishing" has crept in and a reminder of the high points of previous energized and productive times will help bring participants back on target. Identifying what worked, the group plans what they can do personally, identifying a project they are willing to contribute to that will bring them back on target.

Flourishing Communities Worksheet

Lead-In Statement

We live and work in a fast-paced, increasingly complex and interdependent global economy, where the felt need for greater connectivity and communion between people with similar goals, aspirations, and values is growing at an unprecedented pace. Social networking spaces, collaborations, communities of practice, and coalitions are emerging and even co-mingling across territories, disciplines, industries, and demographics. Individuals and groups are attracted to social and professional networks for many reasons, such as companionship, connection, support, learning, professional growth, sharing of knowledge, expertise, and contribution. We have all been members of different communities and networking organizations, some more engaging than others. For now, let's focus on a time when you were part of a flourishing community/organization in which you were fully engaged; you participated in ways you wanted; you shared something of yourself; you were proud of your own contributions; you felt energized by others; and you achieved outcomes that were important to you and the community, so you could say that you contributed to the flourishing of a community.

Focus 1 — Your High-Point Experience in a Flourishing Community/Organization

Paired Interviews

1. Recall a high point or peak experience for you in a flourishing community you are or have been part of. Describe it. Tell your story.
   - What was happening?
   - Who was involved?
   - How did you participate?

> "It is not our purpose to become each other; it is to recognize each other, to learn to see the other and honor him for what he is."
> Hermann Hesse
> (1877–1962)

- In what ways was it energizing and engaging and valuable to you?

2. In your high-point story, what are the things you valued most about:

   - Yourself?

   - The intention and nature of the community and its work?

   - Its organization (how it was organized)?

Focus 2—Sharing Stories of Flourishing Communities

Interview Pairs Combine to Form Groups of Four or Six

3. In your small groups, interviewers introduce their interview partners and share highlights of their partners' stories of "Flourishing Communities."

   - As you listen respectfully, focus on the common themes that come up in the stories.

   - Select a story that you all agree reflects most of the common themes and share it with the other groups.

   - Of all the stories you've heard, what are the best or most successful attributes of "Flourishing Communities"—the "positive core"—those factors that make it vibrant, energizing, and satisfying?

4. What are your three wishes for you own community to truly flourish?

Focus 3—Future Possibility: Collective Dream

Group Work

5. You fall into a deep sleep and wake up refreshed … and it's one year later and you are engaged in this community and it is operating at its best.

   - What is going on that engages you fully?

> "A community is like a ship; everyone ought to be prepared to take the helm."
> Henrik Ibsen (1828–1906)

- What is contributing to its success?
- How are you incorporating your strengths—positive core—and your three wishes?

6. In as creative way as possible, describe, draw, or perform a skit that captures the essence of your flourishing community.

Focus 4—Co-Design Your Community

7. As you think and talk about your dream for your flourishing community, what are the key design elements you will include from your dream that will give greater vitality and energy to it? For example:
   - Who are the participants and members?
   - What are the activities?
   - What technologies are you using?
   - What is your stated purpose?
   - What are your articulated values?

8. Select one of the design elements that you know something about or one that you are very interested in knowing more about. Meet with other participants in the room today who are interested in the same element to decide how this element will help your community flourish. In your new group, create a compelling, future possibility statement of how your element will add life, vitality, and energy to your community.

9. Read out, perform, or represent your compelling future possibility statement.

> "Call it a clan, call it a network, call it a tribe, call it a family: Whatever you call it, whoever you are, you need one."
>
> Jane Howard (b. 1923)

10. What excites you most about the future possibility statements?

   - How do they serve you and you serve them?

   - If you were to go forward and be part of a project team, create a broad-brush project plan that you could present to a sponsor for approval.

11. What is the smallest step you can take now that will have the greatest impact?

Peak Performance — Being in Flow

Timing and Process — 3 hours	Benefits and Outcomes
Focus 1 — 40 minutes • 20 minutes for each interview **Focus 2 — 50 minutes** • 30 minutes for groups to share stories • 20 minutes for groups to respond to Q4, including facilitated debriefing **Focus 3 — 50 minutes** • 15 minutes to create statements • 25 minutes to share and receive support and recommendations in dyads or triads • 10 minutes facilitated debriefing **Focus 4 — 30 minutes** • 10 minutes in personal reflection • 10 minutes in groups • 10 minutes facilitated debriefing **Buffer time — 10 minutes for short break and to allow additional time for activities and longer debriefings.**	The aim of this workshop is for participants to share their experiences of peak performance and articulate what being fully engaged — *being in flow* — is for them. To be conscious of such experiences informs us we have been fully absorbed in what we are doing. It is valuable to know what activities, skills, applications of knowledge, or relationships bring on peak performance so we can create the conditions for further peak performance at work or play.

Peak Performance—Being in Flow Worksheet

Lead-In Statement

We have all, independently or as a group, been so engrossed and engaged in an activity that we lose our sense of time. We are fully absorbed and feel such concentration with a deep involvement that the effort is extremely satisfying. It may have been hard, but at the end of the effort, we felt energized. People report feelings of being in a *state of flow*, at one with the experience, as, for example, when an orchestra or band plays music so brilliantly that the audience and musicians are transported. The football team plays as if every move were choreographed and the crowd is right there with them. The planning committee reaches agreement, respectfully addressing the needs of others, creating solutions that all can participate in equally. These teams behave as a single organism with an energy that is collective and contagious. Flow Theory, the psychology of optimal experience, was developed by Mihaly Csikszentmihalyi. "It is easy to enter flow and feel energized in games such as chess, tennis, or poker, because they have goals and rules that make it possible for the player to act without questioning what should be done. Flow also happens when a person's skills are fully involved in overcoming a challenge that is just about manageable, so it acts as a magnet for learning new skills and increasing challenges."

Focus 1—Your High-Peak Flow Experience

Paired Interviews

1. Think back to a time when you had a peak experience when you felt this sense of flow, when you were at one with the experience and there were no boundaries between you and the activity. You felt truly energized and satisfied by what you had done. Please describe your experience.

   - What was happening?

   - Who was involved?

> "… joy, creativity, the process of total involvement with life I call flow."
> Mihaly Csikszentmihalyi
> (b. 1934)

- How did you participate?
- In what ways was it energizing and satisfying?

2. In your story, what was it about you and your effort that made it such an energizing experience?
    - Without being humble, what did you value about yourself in that story?
    - If others were involved, what did you value about them?
    - How did the organization of it help to keep you energized?

Focus 2—Highlights of Peak Performances

Interview Pairs Combine to Form Groups of Four or Six

3. In your small groups, interviewers introduce their interview partners and share highlights of their partners' stories of "peak performance."
    - As you listen respectfully, focus on the common themes that come up in the stories.
    - Select a story that you agree reflects all or most of the common themes and share it with the other groups.

4. Of all the stories you've heard, what factors come across as key to achieving "peak performance"—those factors that seem to bring it on?
    - Is it level of skill, will, challenge, support, belief, conditions? Be as clear as you can about the contributing factors.

Focus 3—Future Scenario: Dream

Individual Reflection Followed by Dyads or Triads to Share Personal Statements and Hear Feedback

5. It is six months into the future and you are invited to be part of a project that is like a dream come true. You didn't think

"Feelings of worth can flourish only in an atmosphere where individual differences are appreciated, mistakes are tolerated, communication is open, and rules are flexible—the kind of atmosphere that is found in a nurturing family."
Virginia Satir (1916–1988)

this would be possible. In fact, it excites you and you want to be part of it.

- What is going on that keeps you fully charged to do your best work so you are totally oblivious to the hours passing while you work in such a flow state?

- What talents and strengths are you integrating into this project?

6. Create a brief personal statement that captures what it is that energizes you. What are you doing?

- What are you feeling?

- What is contributing to your being in that flow state that is so totally consuming?

Focus 4 — Designing the Future Now

Individual Reflection, Followed by a Group Debriefing

7. Knowing what it takes to feel in that flow state, when you are doing your best work, what will help you get there more frequently? Do you need greater or less challenge; fewer or more learning opportunities; increased or decreased autonomy?

8. If you had three wishes to bring on this feeling of peak experience, what would they be?

9. What is an activity you are involved in now or could start almost immediately that you know will energize you?

"The secret of joy in work is contained in one word — excellence. To know how to do something well is to enjoy it."
Pearl S. Buck (1892–1973)

Caring for Our Environment

Timing and Process—2 hours, 55 minutes	Benefits and Outcomes
Focus 1—30 minutes • 15 minutes for each interview **Focus 2—50 minutes** • 30 minutes for groups to share stories and report out the most exemplary story • 10 minutes to facilitate the positive core Q3 • 10 minutes for groups to respond to Q4 **Focus 3—50 minutes** • 30 minutes to create the dream • 10 minutes to present • 10 minutes facilitated debriefing **Focus 4—35 minutes** • 15 minutes in groups • 10 minutes personal reflection and planning • 10 minutes facilitated debriefing **Buffer time—10 minutes for short break and to allow additional time for activities and longer debriefings.**	The benefits of this workshop are in participants sharing their views about taking care of the environment. The conversations will focus on the systemic benefits of sustainable workplaces, communities, families, and individuals. We all have important roles to play. In this workshop, participants identify what the workplace is doing well already in this important area. They share knowledge about how environmental awareness and corporate citizenship are practiced and what more can be done. Increased personal awareness and individual or team action plans on the topic of "Caring for Our Environment" are goals of this workshop.

Caring for Our Environment Worksheet

Lead-In Statement

We have awakened! The time is now to show how much we value our planet and the environment in which we live. Indigenous peoples—the first peoples, the hunter-gatherers, such as Australian Aboriginals, Bushman from Southern Africa, Mayans from South America, and Natives of North Americas—whose survival depended on their relationship with the earth thousands of years ago—tell us that we need to love where we live and treat the Earth with great respect. Our governments and global corporations have awakened too! We have new regulations about reducing the release of toxic chemicals, plastics, hazardous wastes, lethal emissions, and other pollutants into the air, water, and land. We are encouraged to conserve energy by unplugging electrical and gas appliances when we are not using them. We are urged to take our own reusable shopping bags when we go to the store. We are reminded to recycle all we can. We live in exciting times. We have much new information and many new resources that can help us to be creative about helping our planet. We are investing in natural and recyclable energy sources. There are many great examples of companies and people who are doing the right thing now for our plant, Earth.

Focus 1—"Loving Planet Earth" Stories

Paired Interviews

1. As you think about the conversations around global warming, sustainability, and the future of our planet, what's a story that has impacted you? It may be news you've heard that excites you or worries you. It may be something you are personally involved with to create greater awareness of this most significant opportunity of our times. For now, let's focus on a positive story that's impacted you to wake up.

   • What's your story?

"In our every deliberation, we must consider the impact of our decisions on the next seven generations."
From the Great Law of the Iroquois Confederacy

- Who is involved? What's their role, and what are they doing?

- How are you personally attached to this story?

- Have you participated in or are you moved to participate in this activity or something similar?

Focus 2—Our Collective Wake-Up Call

Interview Pairs Combine to Form Groups of Four or Six

2. In your small groups, interviewers introduce their interview partners and share highlights of their partners' wake-up call stories.

   - As you listen respectfully, focus on the common themes that come up in the stories.

   - Select a story that you agree reflects all or most of the common themes about caring for the environment and share it with the other groups.

3. All of the common themes that serve to sustain our planet are key to its future and can be deemed the "positive core" of sustainability efforts. What have you identified from your stories and themes?

4. What are your three wishes for your organization/community to take an even stronger commitment to the environment or the larger community of which is it a part?

Focus 3—Our Aspirations

Small Groups

5. What are your highest aspirations for your local environment (work or home)? What would you like to see more of? Less of? For example:

   - How is waste disposed of?

   - How is energy conserved—water, electricity, gas?

> "Sustainability is not about philanthropy. There's nothing wrong with corporate charity, but the sustainable company conducts its business so that benefits flow naturally to all stakeholders, including employees, customers, business partners, the communities in which it operates, and, of course, shareholders."
>
> Andrew Savitz, author of
> *Triple Bottom Line* (2006)

- What vehicles are on the roads?

- What is the packaging like?

- What about your vendors and suppliers—how environmentally aware are they?

- What are generational perspectives on this topic? What do children teach adults and vice versa?

6. What are you aware of that other organizations/communities/countries are doing to show they truly care for the environment?

7. Present your group's "aspirations" as creatively as you wish to the other groups. It could be a drawing, a collage, a performance, a song, a poem. Be imaginative, informative, and enjoy your performance!

Focus 4—Making a Difference

Group Work

8. Current contribution: Taking into consideration your aspirations and wishes, what opportunities already exist that you can put your mind, heart, and body into? What will you do immediately?

9. Future projects: What new opportunities can you create or be part of? What resources, including other people, will you want to include? What's your timeline for this opportunity? Create a "back of the envelope" project plan.

10. Your results: What results do you want to achieve that will offer the most positive impact to your organization, your community, and even the world?

"So divinely is the world organized that every one of us is in balance with everything else."
Johann Wolfgang von Goethe (1749–1832)

Learning at a New Level

Timing and Process—2 hours, 30 minutes	Benefits and Outcomes
Focus 1—40 minutes • 20 minutes for each interview **Focus 2—45 minutes** • 30 minutes for groups to share stories and report out the exemplary story • 15 minutes to facilitate the common themes followed by the positive core in Q2 **Focus 3—60 minutes** • 20 minutes to reflect and create personal plans • 30 minutes to share plans in small groups, receive feedback to hone the plans • 10 minutes facilitated debriefing **Buffer time—5 minutes for a short break and to allow additional time for activities or debriefings**	The aim of this inquiry is for participants to value all the learning that takes place at work and at leisure and gain some clarity around what environments, subjects, and mental and emotional states support good learning experiences. As a result of such discoveries and insights, participants can position themselves to embrace learning in a more conscious and expansive way in the future and ask for opportunities that will enhance their learning. This workshop is a useful precursor to a performance appraisal.

Learning at a New Level Worksheet

Lead-In Statement

Whether you are a student, teacher, volunteer, employee, or CEO, you know what it's like to experience excitement and satisfaction when you are learning something new and you feel energized by it and can apply yourself to it. Very often, it creates in you a strong desire to stretch yourself and go that extra mile because you can see the value in what you are doing. You experience learning at a whole new level. It is exciting and worth the effort.

Focus 1 — Your High-Peak Learning Experience

Paired Interviews

1. Tell your story about a time you were highly engaged and excited when working on a project or activity, in which you were learning something new and were fully absorbed. You were supported by those around you and felt a sense of energy and excitement about the activity. The learning was both exciting and challenging. Please tell your story.

   - What was the project or activity?

   - What was the learning for you?

   - Who else was involved? What were their roles and how did they contribute?

   - What made this a good learning experience for you? What factors contributed?

2. Without being humble, what did you value about yourself as you applied your full effort to learning? What were the most important contributing factors, and what are your personal

> "Do all the good you can, by all the means you can, in all the ways you can, in all the places you can, at all the times you can, to all the people you can, as long as ever you can."
>
> John Wesley (1703–1791)

strengths that engaged you fully and helped you accomplish what you set out to do?

3. How did this experience encourage you to pursue your interests and become involved with other projects that required you to learn more?

   - Did you go on to do more of that same type of learning?

   - What are some of the consequences from that learning—increased responsibilities, more challenges, greater excitement, promotion, new opportunities?

   - What rewards did you enjoy, whether intrinsic and extrinsic?

4. Who else or what else can you be grateful for in this powerful learning experience? For example, were you supported in some way that really helped?

Focus 2—Sharing Stories of Learning at a New Level

Interview Pairs Combine to Form Groups of Four or Six

5. In small groups, interviewers introduce their interview partners and share highlights of their partners' stories of "learning at a new level."

   - As you listen respectfully, focus on the common themes that come up in the stories.

   - Select a story that you agree reflects all or most of the common themes and share it with the other groups.

6. Select one story that exemplifies the topic of focused learning. What are those factors that make it vibrant, energizing, and satisfying—the "positive core"—that are transferable from one learning experience to the next?

"Leadership and learning are indispensable to each other."
John F. Kennedy
(1917–1963)

> "I would rather have a mind opened by wonder than one closed by belief."
> Gerry Spence (b. 1929)

Focus 3 — Sustaining Learning at a New Level

Individual Reflection Followed by Group Debriefing

7. What types of experiences do you need to keep on learning at a new level?

   - How can these experiences happen at work to keep you learning?
   - How will you create those experiences for yourself?
   - Who do you need to involve?

8. What is the first action you can take to learn something new that excites you?

Working with Integrity

Note for Facilitators: Although this workshop focuses on the value "integrity", you could select any organizational value. You could also facilitate this workshop with every value the organization holds, allowing participants to discover and learn together the range of perspectives across teams and to collect positive stories about the application of each of the values. The end result would be a wonderful collection of stories that could be included in a corporate blog or newsletter.

Timing and Process—4 hours, 5 minutes	Benefits and Outcomes
Focus 1—40 minutes • 20 minutes for each interview **Focus 2—60 minutes** • 40 minutes for groups to share stories and report out an exemplary story • 20 minutes to respond to Q4 followed by facilitated debriefing **Focus 3—65 minutes** • 30 minutes to create the dream • 10 minutes to present • 25 minutes for uplifting statements, including report out and facilitated debriefing **Focus 4—40 minutes** • 20 minutes in groups • 20 minutes facilitated debriefing around Q8 and Q9 **Focus 5—30 minutes** • 10 minutes for personal reflection • 10 minutes of group conversation • 10 minutes facilitated debriefing **Buffer time—10 minutes for short break and allow additional time for activities and longer debriefings.**	The purpose of this workshop is for participants to have important and meaningful conversations around organizational values. The outcome is that they will be very clear about how the values are lived out day in and day out. They will know who is and who is not living up to the values. The value "integrity" is showcased here. It is a significant one, especially as history has shown it is a challenging one to uphold. If cynicism and doubt are voiced too often, the conversation can change to unresourceful blame and shame mode. That does not help in moving toward what we want in upholding values.

Working with Integrity Worksheet

Lead-In Statement

Knowing what values you hold in life provides a compass that helps you stay the course. Until you do some reflection to name those values that are really important to you, you most likely will make decisions based on your unconscious beliefs. Values are important determinants of human emotions, thoughts, and behaviors. Furthermore, we default to our values when faced with uncertainty and when confronted by the unknown. Understanding what is important to ourselves and others is the first step in beginning to appreciate each other. How we view and interpret the world is based on our historical-cultural perspectives that form our beliefs and our values. As they say, "Beauty lies in the eyes of the beholder." How you interpret beauty is likely to be different from my interpretation of it. Neither one of us is right or wrong. Both of us have valid perspectives. If we explore our different perspectives on "beauty," then we might come to a new perspective and together we will have co-constructed an expanded view of beauty. The same goes for "respect," "teamwork," "service," "empathy," "integrity," "honesty," and "caring." These are all commonly held organizational values. You often see them framed in front offices. Today, we will focus on the value "integrity."

Focus 1 — Stories of Integrity

Paired Interviews

1. "Integrity" is one of those complex constructs that at its root is about being whole, intact, unfragmented, and uncorrupted. We talk about the integrity of a piece of music or a forest when each is in its pure form. A similar meaning has spilled over to human behavior. When we refer to human beings as having integrity, we view them as whole, true to themselves, consistent, and untainted. In this light,

"To be free from all egoistic motive, careful of truth in speech and action, void of self-will and self-assertion, watchful in all things, is the condition for being a flawless servant."

Sri Aurobindo (1872–1950)

"integrity" is a character virtue and is thus a strength. From this stance, recall a time when you were aware that "integrity" was lived out in your organization. How was it demonstrated? What was its effect? Please tell your story.

- What was the situation?
- Who was involved?
- What things were said and done?
- What behaviors were evident?
- What emotions were visible?
- How did you feel as an initiator, a participant, or as an observer?

2. What really stood out at the time and has had a lasting impact on you, and to your knowledge, a lasting impact on others?

Focus 2—High Points of Stories of "Integrity"

Interview Pairs Combine to Form Groups of Four or Six

3. In your small groups, interviewers introduce their interview partners and share the stories they heard. As you listen, be aware of the impact these stories have on you.

- How does it feel to listen to someone else retell your story about integrity?
- Select the highlights of your collective stories and report out to the other groups in the room one of your stories that seems to capture most of the ideas.

4. Reflecting on all the stories now, what common themes come through? What are some of the most powerful examples of "integrity" in your organization—your organization's positive core?

- How is it demonstrated internally and externally?
- What can you be proud of in your organization?

> "Beauty, truth, friendship, love, creation: these are the great values of life. We can't prove them, or explain them, yet they are the most stable things in our lives."
> Jesse Herman Holmes
> (1864–1942)

Focus 3 — Aspirations and Opportunities

Continue in Small Groups as Above

5. Taking your existing examples of "integrity," imagine what else is possible as you live with integrity. What else inspires you, remembering how important and meaningful integrity is to you, your organization, customers, your families, and all other stakeholders? Think about other opportunities and possibilities to make integrity even stronger. Imagine it is two years from today; you've been on a long sabbatical. You return to your office to find that integrity has been truly upheld while you were absent.

   - What are you seeing in your organization two years into the future?

   - What business is being transacted? What services, products? How and with whom?

   - How are your customers and vendors responding?

   - What behaviors most commonly demonstrate the strength of "integrity" in your organization?

   - How are people communicating? What is the tone of the language you are hearing? What expressions do you see?

6. In a creative way, present your aspirations to the other groups. It could be a song, skit, media interview, picture, poem — have fun with it.

7. Create an uplifting statement that integrates the shared perspectives played out in the presentations, highlighting the purpose and focus of integrity, coming from your positive core.

"We make a living by what we get, but we make a life by what we give."
Winston Churchill
(1874–1965)

Focus 4—Resources and Results

Group Work

8. To live up to the future image you have, what resources might you need? Is there technology involved, or communications, or training, or further investments? How will leadership support you? How will you support leadership? Please share your recommendations.

9. Once you are clear about what it means and what it takes, what results do you expect?

   - For you personally at work?

   - For the team, the organization, the community?

   - How will you know your value is being lived out?

Focus 5—Group and Personal Reflection

10. Reflect on the alignment of "integrity" in your personal life with that in your work life.

    - How do you live with integrity outside of work. Share some of your personal stories.

    - Where is it in synch and where is there a misfit, if at all, between the two?

    - What can you do from today forward to show your commitment to live with integrity?

> "Personality can open doors, but only character can keep them open."
>
> Elmer G. Letterman
> (1897–1982)

Purpose-Driven Selling

Timing and Process — 4 hours, 15 minutes	Benefits and Outcomes
Focus 1 — 40 minutes • 20 minutes for each interview **Focus 2 — 55 minutes** • 30 minutes for groups to share stories • 15 minutes to facilitate the positive core (Q4) after group discussion • 10 minutes for groups to respond to Q5, including facilitated feedback **Focus 3 — 60 minutes** • 30 minutes to create the dream • 10 minutes to present • 20 minutes to respond to Q7, including facilitated debriefing **Focus 4 — 55 minutes** • 45 minutes to design group project • 10 minutes facilitated debriefing **Focus 5 — 30 minutes** • 10 minutes in groups • 10 minutes facilitated debriefing • 5 minutes personal reflection • 5 minutes facilitated debriefing **Buffer time — 15 minutes for short break and allow additional time for activities and longer debriefings.**	The aim of workshop is to celebrate the role and contribution of sales professionals. A little investment in sharing high-point stories of past experiences and taking the best of the past into the future is a strengthening activity. The outcome of this session is to create a plan aligning individual successes and strengths with organizational strengths to achieve and deliver on visions of continued future success.

Purpose-Driven Selling Worksheet

Lead-In Statement

Knowing yourself well—your strengths, your skills, motivations, values, beliefs, and all the other positive attributes that energize you—is the gateway to great performance. When you feel upbeat and energized, your relationships with everyone else flow so much more effortlessly and are more satisfying, rewarding, and sustainable. It is the same when you represent your company. By staying positively centered in every interaction and emphasizing the strengths of your products and services rather than being evasive or apologetic, or worse, downgrading the competition, you maintain an integrity that will serve you. Equally important is having the knowledge of and belief in the product, service, and organization you represent. Having confidence that your company culture reinforces strong ethics and morality and supports you to do right by your customer is an assurance you are on the best path toward creating trusting, long-term relationships. Furthermore, when you know that your colleagues and your management are aligned in their willingness to help one another, perhaps through sharing knowledge, learning, and encouragement, it contributes to a positive work ethic which results in mutual benefits.

Focus 1—Discover Best Stories

1. We have all, at some time or another, been part of a successful, rewarding selling experience, whether it was selling a pretty pink lipstick, a million-dollar service contract, or tickets to your local arts fund-raising dinner. Reflect on a time when you felt at your best in a selling situation. Everything seemed perfectly aligned—timing, customers, your knowledge and message, the questions, and how you managed your responses, and so forth. Tell your story.

   • What was the situation?

> "A successful individual typically sets his next goal somewhat but not too much above his last achievement. In this way he steadily raises his level of aspiration."
>
> Kurt Lewin (1890–1947)

- What was the purpose?
- Who was there?
- What was the outcome?
- How did you feel?

2. Without being modest, what do you value about yourself in your story?

- What do you value about the work you were doing?
- What did you value about the organizations—yours and your customer's?

Focus 2—Highlights of All Stories

Interview Pairs Combine to Form Groups of Four or Six

3. In your small groups, interviewers introduce their interview partners and share highlights of their partners' stories of a purpose-driven sales experience.

- As you listen respectfully, focus on the common themes that come up in the stories.

> "Treat people as if they were what they ought to be and you help them to become what they are capable of being."
>
> Goethe (1749–1832)

4. Select a story that exemplifies the strengths, best assets, and successes in a sales experience to share with all other groups.

- What are the collective strengths across all the stories? What are you all doing successfully? Those collective strengths are your "positive core."

5. What wishes do you have to further strengthen your selling performance?

Focus 3—Dream: What More Is Possible?

Small Group Work

6. Let's assume that tonight you go into a deep sleep and you wake up one year from now and go back into the field and you are selling products and services you are proud of with

colleagues you admire. The relationships with your clients are really strong and you are exceeding your sales targets.

- What does that look like?
- Who are your customers? Are they internal or external?
- What's happening?
- What product or service are you selling?
- What are the things that made it happen?
- How can you play to the perceived strengths of your customers?
- What possibilities exist that the customers may not yet have considered?
- What differentiates you? Why should your customers believe in you?
- What is the customer's current perception of you and your organization?
- How have your wishes come true?
- What makes this dream exciting?

7. Present your group's dream as creatively as you wish to the other groups. It could be a drawing, a collage, a performance, a song, a poem. Be imaginative and perform well!

8. Capture the essence of your dream in an uplifting statement or two.

Focus 4—Design: Co-Designing Your New Reality

Group Work

9. Take your dream statement that you just created and begin to make it real: translate it into goals, strategies, action items, and so on. Consider the following:

- Whom are you specifically targeting?
- What specific services or products are you selling?

"Sales are contingent upon the attitude of the salesman—not the attitude of the prospect."
W. Clement Stone
(1902–2002)

- What solutions are you offering?

- In what times frames and in what volume? What are some milestones you can set?

- What three benefits will customers gain from your service? How will you know when you have succeeded?

10. Create a project plan that you can implement with objectives, action plans, roles, responsibilities, time lines, and measures.

Focus 5—Destiny: Sustaining the Success

Personal Reflection and Sharing

11. What will help you keep track of your achievements? How will you sustain the enthusiasm and excitement of your valuable contribution, knowing that we all have great days and not-so-great days?

12. What will you commit to so that you continue to learn more, build on your skills, adapt to changes, and improvise when the situation calls for it?

Global Interconnectivity

Timing and Process—4 hours, 15 minutes	Benefits and Outcomes
Focus 1—30 minutes • 15 minutes for each interview **Focus 2—30 minutes** • 20 minutes for groups to share stories • 10 minutes for groups to respond to Q3, including facilitated debriefing **Focus 3—65 minutes** • 30 minutes to create the dream • 10 minutes to present • 15 minutes for future possibility statement • 10-minute debriefing after Q5 **Focus 4—60 minutes** • 30 minutes in groups to discuss and create four lists • 30 minutes to consolidate Q8, followed by facilitated debriefing **Focus 5—60 minutes** • 30 minutes in groups to discuss and create plans for Q9, Q10, and Q11 • 20 minutes to report out Q12, followed by facilitated debriefing • 10 minutes for facilitated closing Q13 **Buffer time—10 minutes for short break and to allow additional time for activities and longer debriefings.**	This workshop is an opportunity for participants to value the role technology plays in connecting us globally and to imagine future possibilities that will extend the benefits. Furthermore, here is an opportunity for information technology and Internet professionals to collaborate with their internal and external customers. Taking a whole systems and totally democratic perspective facilitating all voices that need and want to be heard, they come together to co-design platforms and applications that will serve and deliver the best solutions to benefit all. The most heartening and empowering outcome is to pay attention to the wise application of such technologies.

Global Interconnectivity Worksheet

Lead-In Statement

In our global, interconnected world, social media tools, and information technology are increasingly key enablers for organizations, associations, communities, and institutions to perform at their best, live up to their highest purpose and values, execute on strategy, achieve their goals and operational excellence, engage stakeholders across the world, and create value innovatively and extensively. Web-based tools and information technology serve to streamline operations, accelerate the speed of connection, greatly enhance the opportunities for collective knowledge sharing and new knowledge creation, and facilitate shared ownership and problem solving, thereby adding value and meaning to the technological experience. Partnering with web-based providers and IT associates to build a dynamic platform for global connectivity is how we operate in the world today. Moreover, as long as the web remains open to all, it provides access to all, without discrimination based on politics, economics, gender, race, or religion. It is open to all to share stories, passions, dreams, knowledge, practical wisdom, hopes, and aspirations. It allows more voices than ever before to be heard.

Focus 1 — Exciting Stories of Web-Enabled Connections

Paired Interviews

1. What have you or others experienced through an IT system or a web-based application that had an empowering outcome for all involved? It may have been at work or school, or through a community of practice or social networking group you belong to.

   - What was the situation and how did it begin?

"I do not fear computers. I fear the lack of them."
Isaac Asimov (1920–1992)

- Describe the process and what emerged for you as your experience developed and strengthened through this medium.

- What did you do, and how did you feel at times?

- What made it a successful experience for you or your group?

Focus 2 — Highlights of Stories

Interview Pairs Combine to Form Groups of Four or Six

2. In your small groups, interviewers introduce their interview partners and share highlights of their partners' stories of "global interconnectivity."

   - As you listen respectfully, focus on the common themes that come up in the stories.

   - Select a story that you agree reflects all or most of the common themes and share it with the other groups.

3. Of all the stories you've heard, what are the best or most successful examples of "global interconnectivity"? What factors excite you about IT and/or web-enabled possibilities for human-to-human, business-to-business, and human-to-computer connectivity?

Focus 3 — Imagine the Possibilities

Group Work

4. We have come so far in such a short time. Already we have a generation that doesn't know a world without the web. To think of businesses, hospitals, schools, entertainment and day-to-day communications without the web is impossible now. With more than a generation of experience to build on

> "When we seek for connection, we restore the world to wholeness. Our seemingly separate lives become meaningful as we discover how truly necessary we are to each other."
>
> Margaret Wheatley

and learn from, what initiatives do you think would serve us all even more—in our workplaces, whether corporations, hospitals, schools, government, local communities, or homes? Imagine you fall into a deep sleep tonight and that, when you wake up, it's five years into the future. Information and web-based technologies have merged and morphed in such exciting ways. What are you now experiencing in this technology-enabled world five years into the future?

- Describe this new world of your dreams in words, pictures, or prepare a media presentation or a performance that includes all the things you want to see.

- What is making it a better world for all?

- Creatively, present your imagined interconnected new world to the other groups.

5. Capture the essence of your presentation and in a sentence or two write it as a statement of future possibility.

Focus 4—Designing the New Technologies

Group Work

6. Here is where unfettered imagination and on-the-ground experience come together. Take your dream statement and together co-design a roadmap to get there.

- What will you keep because it works well right now and will continue to support your vision?

- What will you dump because it's old technology and no longer serves a purpose?

- What will you create that's necessary and doable right now?

- What will you keep in the interim because it's too soon to let go of, for example, you may have budget constraints, skills gaps, or some other variables that require you to hang on to the old while you transition or migrate to the new.

- You will end up with four lists: Keep, Dump, Create, Transition.

7. Report out to the other groups the content of your four lists.

8. Consolidate the ideas from each of the four categories across groups, so you end up with only one list of each of the four categories.

Focus 5 — Destiny: Continuous Connection

Individual, Work Groups, and Reflection

9. Select a project you could work on with some passion.

- What would you want to contribute?

- What's your role and responsibility, the time frames, success measures? What other resources might you need?

10. Find other participants in the room today who are interested in the same IT-related/web project. In your new design group, create a compelling future possibility statement of how your project will add life, vitality, and energy to your organization.

11. How will you maintain the interest and momentum to ensure the dream stays alive and that there is continued energy for it? Create some short, quick wins to keep the interest high while you develop your pathways toward your longer-term goals. Which of these types of initiative might serve you as you build toward the long term?

- How do you create a match between needs and offerings?

- How do you contribute your learnings and experiences?

- How do you attract new users to participate and share?

- How do you teach the willing and interested?

- What are your next steps?

12. Share your high-level project plans with other groups so you all get a sense of what you have the will and the ability to create.

13. How has today's workshop facilitated your awareness of what's possible? What have you learned about working together to make it happen?

Generations Working Together

Timing and Process—3 hours	Benefits and Outcomes
Focus 1—40 minutes • 20 minutes for each interview **Focus 2—40 minutes** • 20 minutes for groups to share stories • 10 minutes to facilitate the positive core Q4 • 10 minutes facilitated discussion of Q5 **Focus 3—60 minutes** • 30 minutes to create the dream • 10 minutes to present • 10 minutes Q10 • 10 minutes facilitated debriefing **Focus 4—30 minutes** • 20 minutes facilitated group discussion Q11 through Q14 • 5 minutes for individual reflection • 5 minutes facilitated debriefing **Buffer time—10 minutes for short break and to allow additional time for activities and longer debriefings.**	In this workshop, you will need a group representative of the different generations, or at least some "old" and "young" (which is an interesting choice in and of itself—something worth exploring in the workshop. What constitutes "old" and what constitutes "young"?). The purpose is to have cross-generational conversations to hear each other, learn about each other, and focus on those factors that contribute to shared understanding and good relationships. The goal is to identify the best of each generation present and determine how that can be leveraged at work to create generative outcomes.

Generations Working Together Worksheet

Lead-In Statement

What are the stereotypes we attach to the different generations? If you generalized, how might you complete these sentences? Old people are … . Young people are … . If you have difficulty generalizing, that's a good thing, as we are all unique and different. It appears our world is moving toward greater tolerance in many things—cultures, age groups, working styles. Fashion and music seem to lead the way. Moreover, movies and YouTube videos from all over the world are available to us 24/7, so we are more exposed to and welcoming of difference. We see bright young people doing amazing things with games and technology and music and movement. We see interested old people who have energy and sparkle, curious about everything, sharing their stories and insights of earlier times. When we stop to think about it, there is so much to admire in all the generations. Imagine the power of having such an open perspective at all times—understanding and appreciation would make conversations so much easier and more generative. When we let go of judgment, we achieve so much more because we focus on what works, instead of investing energy into stereotyping people based on traditional assumptions or prejudices.

Focus 1—Memorable Cross-Generational Stories

Paired Interviews

1. Remember a positive experience you had with a person from a different generation. The situation may have been at work or at home, on the street, or anywhere. This positive experience shifted your perspectives about this generation,

"We did not change as we grew older; we just became more clearly ourselves."

Lynn Hall (b. 1937)

different from yours, in a new way that was helpful and left you feeling good. Describe what happened.

- Tell your story.

- Who was involved?

- What were you doing?

- What did you say to each other, or what were you observing?

2. Without being humble, what were some of the specific things about you that made this a positive experience? What are some things you did, thought, and felt? What about this experience engenders some pride?

3. What about the other person or persons? What did you value about them? What's fun or different or uniquely special about this other generation? What made you shift your perspective?

Focus 2—High Points of Stories

Interview Pairs Combine to Form Groups of Four or Six

4. In your small groups, interviewers introduce their interview partners and share highlights of their partners' stories of "Generations Working Together."

- As you listen respectfully, focus on the common themes that come up in the stories.

- Select a story that you agree reflects all or most of the common themes and share it with the other groups.

- Of all the stories you've heard, what are the best or most successful encounters between generations—a "positive

> "The greatest discovery of my generation is that a human being can alter his life by altering his attitudes of mind."
> William James (1842–1910)

core"—those factors that make intergenerational relationships vibrant, satisfying, and rewarding?

5. From the collective stories you've heard about relating with different generations, what are some of the common themes? What sorts of conditions have to be present for good outcomes?

Focus 3 — Making It Possible

Group Work

6. Building on your themes of what will contribute to good communications across all generations and imagining you had a magic wand to grant yourself three wishes, what would those wishes be for you and for the people of your generation?

7. What are three wishes you would grant for other generations?

8. What are three wishes you would grant for your community or organization?

9. Create a future scene of how you imagine this to be possible. You can draw, sing, dance, or write a poem or prose. Include your collective ideas. Show how you can integrate the best attributes of the different generations. Be prepared to present your scene to the other groups.

10. Take all your creative work and capture its meaning and energy into one or two sentences that communicate your group's admiration for all generations.

Focus 4 — Sticking with It

Group Work and Personal Reflection

11. What insights have you had today about "respecting all generations"?

"I truly believe that if we put the strength of our hearts and minds together that we can change prejudice, and that my generation of kids can grow up appreciating the glorious rainbow of diversity. We have become not a melting pot but a beautiful mosaic. Different people, different beliefs, different yearnings, different hopes, different dreams."
Jimmy Carter (b. 1924)

12. Of the ways you work and interact, what are the things you will keep doing because it works for everybody and the organization?

13. What are some things that you will need to be sensitive to as you continue to pay attention to respecting generations other than your own; and what do you need to be sensitive to when you notice others who are perhaps not as insightful or aware as you are?

14. What new attitudes or behaviors will you demonstrate because you know they will help make a positive difference?

15. Name one behavior that you will commit to take on and continue to be mindful of how that works for you and others.

Juggling It All!

Timing and Process—3 hours, 15 minutes	Benefits and Outcomes
Focus 1—40 minutes • 20 minutes for each interview **Focus 2—50 minutes** • 30 minutes for groups to share stories • 10 minutes to facilitate the positive core • 10 minutes for groups to respond to Q5 and Q6 with facilitated debriefing **Focus 3—45 minutes** • 20 minutes to create the dream • 15 minutes to present • 10 minutes facilitated debriefing **Focus 4—45 minutes** • 30 minutes to strategize in twos or threes • 15 minutes facilitated debriefing of Q11 and Q12 **Buffer time—15 minutes for short break and to allow additional time for activities and longer debriefings.**	This workshop is suitable for anyone who wants to rethink how he or she relates to time, tasks, and people. Participants will review a past time when they felt "in charge" and "in control." They consider what factors led to this feeling, and distinguish between the internal and external influences over their relationships with time. Once they clarify what they do well, they imagine living a life of being in a balanced relationship with time and strategize ways to achieve such a relationship.

Juggling It All! Worksheet

Lead-In Statement

"Yesterday's the past, tomorrow's the future, but today is a gift. That's why it's called the present."

—Bil Keane (b. 1922)

Work/life balance comes up frequently as a wish for many people, especially if they have the responsibilities of a family and work a full-time job. Even without a family, allocating appropriate resources to all our duties and responsibilities can be challenging and seem to leave very little room for self-time or recreational pursuits. Picture yourself being able to complete all your tasks and responsibilities to your standards and satisfaction and having time and energy left over, so you can enjoy "self-time." It is important for a sane mind, healthy body, and emotional well-being to follow hobbies, learn new things, or just "be," savoring simple down-time. It is scientifically proven that when people are in positive emotional states (as opposed to anxious, fearful, or stressed), they are more hopeful and optimistic, are more able to socially connect well with others, make decisions more rationally, show interest, be grateful and appreciative, and feel generally uplifted (Fredrickson & Branigan, 2005). To appreciate each day as a gift is a worthy goal. It is extremely difficult to achieve that goal alone. We can have the best intentions and be personally well organized, but outside influences impact us and require us to respond. How we respond is a clue to our relationships to time and our ability to juggle it all.

Focus 1

Conditions for Feeling in Balance

1. Even though it seems we may spend more time striving for balance than time when we actually experience balance, there will have been times when you truly have felt calm and at peace with a situation. It may have been the way things unfolded for you at the time, or you engineered the situation in such a way as to make all things work for you. It doesn't matter. There were things about that situation that enabled you to feel in a state of balance. Consider all the factors that contributed to that feeling of being calm, in a peaceful state—instead of panic or stress. What was that experience like? Tell your story.

2. What facilitated your sense of being calm and tranquil?

   - Your skill sets?

   - Your level of knowledge?

   - Resources available at the time?

   - Your own attitude?

   - Beliefs?

   - Desires?

   - Encouragement from others?

   - What was the emotion you felt?

   - What thoughts did you think?

   - What else may have helped?

3. What were the most significant conditions that supported your balanced state?

   - Having or arranging to have help?

   - Your state of mind?

   - Your priorities or the priorities of others?

> "Order is not pressure which is imposed on society from without, but an equilibrium which is set up from within."
> Jose Ortega y Gasset
> (1883–1955)

Focus 2 — Valuing All Stories

Interview Pairs Combine to Form Groups of Four or Six

4. In your small groups, interviewers introduce their interview partners and share highlights of their partners' stories of "feeling in balance."

   - As you listen respectfully, focus on the common themes that come up in the stories.
   - Select a story that you agree reflects all or most of the common themes and share it with the other groups.

5. Of all the stories you've heard, what are the best or most successful attributes of "feeling in balance"—its "positive core"—those factors that enabled you and those around you to remain calm, productive, kind, caring, and positive?

6. From all the stories you've heard, what are some new ideas or strategies that you could add to your repertoire to strengthen your own toolkit?

Focus 3 — Imagine the Balanced Life

Group Conversations and Individual Reflection and Creative Act

7. Change starts first in our imaginations. If you can visualize your balanced life first, you will have clarity about what inner and outer resources will help you achieve what it is you want to create. Describe what you imagine a balanced life would be and represent it as a drawing poem, song, role play—be creative and have fun as you create your ability to juggle it all. Be sure to reveal what feelings come up for you as you imagine your work/life in balance and share them with the group.

> "The future is an infinite succession of presents, and to live now as we think human beings should live, in defiance of all that is bad around us, is itself a marvelous victory."
>
> Howard Zinn (b. 1922)

Focus 4—Designing Your Balanced Life

Individual Reflection with Group Debriefings

"Each time you look at a tangerine, you can see deeply into it. You can see everything in the universe in one tangerine. When you peel it and smell it, it is wonderful. You can take your time eating a tangerine and be very happy."

Thich Nhat Hanh (b. 1926)

8. What can you do to bring your imagined dream to reality? What will you continue to do the same because you do it well or because it works well for you?

9. What new behaviors or attitudes do you need to adopt because you feel confident they will serve you well?

10. What will you ask of others to support you—your work colleagues, your boss, your family members, your friends? Who else or what else would be helpful?

11. What have you gained from this workshop on work/life balance? What does "juggling it all" mean to you now?

12. What is the smallest change you can make that will have the greatest impact?

Reference

Fredrickson, B.L., & Branigan, C. (2005). Positive emotions broaden the scope of attention and though-action repertoires. *Cognition and Emotion, 19*(3), 313–332.

Building Capacity Through Strengths

Timing and Process — 3 hours, 20 minutes	Benefits and Outcomes
Focus 1 — 40 minutes • 20 minutes for each interview **Focus 2 — 60 minutes** • 30 minutes for groups to share stories • 30 minutes to facilitate Q4 through Q6 **Focus 3 — 50 minutes** • 30 minutes to create the dream • 10 minutes to present • 10 minutes facilitated debriefing **Focus 4 — 45 minutes** • 15 minutes in groups Q8 and Q9 • 15 minutes facilitated debriefing • 5 minutes personal reflection Q10 • 10 minutes facilitated debriefing **Buffer time — 5 minutes for short break and to allow additional time for activities and longer debriefings.**	The aim of this workshop is to clarify how working to one's strengths improves satisfaction and productivity and builds organizational capacity. Participants validate that acknowledgment of good performance in real time positively impacts future performance. They create a future scenario that demonstrates how a strength-based organization might operate and identify their own contributions to making it happen.

Building Capacity Through Strengths Worksheet

Lead-In Statement

The maxim "people support what they create" is just as applicable to measuring results and valuing performance in organizational contexts as to other aspects of human endeavors. You know how good you feel when you are acknowledged for doing something worthwhile, when you are praised for achievement, when you are applauded for your contribution or performance. When that happens, you are more inclined to do more of the same with an increased sense of satisfaction. In fact, it is probably hard to stop you doing what you are doing, as we all do our best work and are most productive when we are energized and engaged by the activity. If we are energized rather than depleted, it is likely that we are working with our talents or potential strengths and that the activity itself engages us—we are absorbed in it. Moreover, having the right tools, resources, processes, systems, structures, and supportive people is just as important in helping us achieve our best performance. If you can develop conscious awareness of how frequently you are using your strengths on a daily basis, you will begin to appreciate what contributes to your good performance, that is, your own high levels of productivity and engagement. Moreover, you will be able to see how your strengths line up with what your organization values and its vision, mission, and goals.

Focus 1—Acknowledgment

Paired Interviews

1. Remember a time when you, on your own or on a team, achieved a goal or completed a project and the results were acknowledged, inspiring you to do even better next time.

   - Tell your story.
   - Describe the situation.

"The secret of joy in work is contained in one word—excellence. To know how to do something well is to enjoy it."
Pearl S. Buck (1882–1973)

- What were you doing?
- What was it about and who was involved?
- What kept you going?
- What thoughts and feelings did you have?

2. What strengths—talents or skills—did you bring to the situation?

   - What was specifically acknowledged and how?
   - If it was a team effort, what strengths did you observe in others?
   - What did you value about others' strengths?
   - What did you value about the organization?

Focus 2—What Supports Your Best Work?

Interview Pairs Combine to Form Groups of Four or Six

3. In your small groups, interviewers introduce their interview partners and share highlights of their partners' stories of "acknowledgment."

   - As you listen respectfully, focus on the common themes and strengths that come up in the stories.
   - Select a story that you agree reflects all or most of the common themes and strengths. Share this story with the other groups.

4. Of all the stories you've heard, what are the strengths of this group, both individually and organizationally—the "positive core"—those indicators of what contributes to making this organization vibrant, energizing, and a satisfying place to work?

5. Individually, what percentage of your week do you currently spend in working to your strengths?

6. What three things would enable you to work even more to your strengths?

"The effective executive builds on strengths—their own strengths, the strengths of superiors, colleagues, subordinates; and on the strengths of the situation."
Peter Drucker (1909–2005)

Focus 3—Imagine Working to Your Strengths to Achieve Organizational Excellence

Group Work

7. Imagine you go on family leave for ten months and you come back to work to find that in your absence an Appreciative Inquiry summit has been planned because organizational members requested that a strength-based culture be introduced. Fortunately, you have just returned in time to participate actively in the summit. You and your colleagues are actively engaged in co-designing this highly collaborative and energizing way of working. In your small group, incorporate your collective strengths to design how you want the organization to operate as a strength-based organization. Present your imagined new workplace as creatively as you can—as a performance, a song, a poem, a picture, a metaphor—however you can best convey your dream!

   - Show how you will work to ensure that all members are working to their strengths and bringing best results to themselves, their teams, and the organization.

   - Include new relevant HR policies, technologies, office layouts, operations, ways of measuring performance—whatever else you think is important—that will help such a positive transformation. Remember to express the feelings and benefits of working to one's strengths.

Focus 4—What's Achievable?

Group Conversation and Individual Reflection

8. What have you learned about strengths today?

9. What would you say to your boss/team members about the value of working to one's strengths? Together create a

> "I was always looking outside myself for strength and confidence, but it comes from within. It is there all the time."
>
> Anna Freud (1895–1982)

statement about the value of aligning individual strengths to build organizational capacity and how that would help you to achieve personal and organizational objectives.

10. What are you motivated to do as a result of participating in today's workshop?

Designing Your Own Strength-Based Workshops

Introduction

Part IV provides guidance and support to help you, as a facilitator, dive a little more deeply into the process, principles, and practices of Appreciative Inquiry so you continue to experiment and grow in designing and delivering your own workshops. Most importantly, as you continue to work with this methodology, you are executing the fourth "D" of the 4-D Cycle—the Destiny phase—for you and your constituents: how you claim your own destiny and sustain the momentum of the energy and excitement that is born out of the Appreciative workshops you facilitate from Part III of the book.

By following the guidelines in this section, you will build consistency and continuity into your work as you creatively do your part to help to develop individuals and strengthen your organization's capacity. Here is an opportunity to prototype—to try your hand at designing workshops integrating all that you have learned through reading the earlier parts of the book, especially Part II, and the insights you gained as you facilitated the workshops in Part III.

By the end of this section, you will have reviewed the elements that will enable you to design your own strength-based workshops and trainings, including creating affirmative topics of strategic importance and crafting accompanying interview protocols to help participants strengthen their own capacities and, at the same time align their strengths with organizational strengths. Moreover, you will become aware of further applications for strength-based work.

Review of Workshop Design

Defining the Affirmative Topic

Remember, the affirmative topic is the entry point to any Appreciative Inquiry piece of work. It focuses the change agenda. If knowledge and organization destiny are as intricately interwoven as we think, then it is most likely that the seeds of change are implicit in the very first questions we ask. The traditional approach to training and organization development has been to start from a problem analysis. Appreciative Inquiry takes the view that many things in the system work well already, so the focus is directed to what further possibilities can be imagined to strengthen the system. How you define the topic for inquiry is key.

As the chosen topic is the focus of the inquiry for your organizational members, you will plan your inquiry around a topic of strategic importance or issue critical to the group and its goals. Inquiry topics indicate the direction the organization wants to move toward—the powerful entity it believes it can become. We move in the direction of what we most frequently and systematically ask questions about. So it is preferable to ask what we can do, rather than what we cannot do. As stated previously, the affirmative topic states *what we want*.

Following are some guidelines on how to create an affirmative topic for your own organization's inquiry. For example, if you invite two groups of participants to inquire into the following topics:

- Analysis into low morale or

- Inquiry into engaged alignment,

you will discover two very different stories. The language will be different, the tone different, the energy different, the results different. One topic can set people off on a downward spiral, more likely to de-energize participants by focusing on negative causes, defensive behaviors, and possibly even apportioning blame; while the other topic can set people off on an upward spiral, inviting them to discover times when they experienced or observed fullest engagement, causing them to feel more positive, empowered, and socially connected to others. Moreover, the appreciatively constructed topic focuses the conversation on what they want to produce, the very act of *participating* is *producing* the solution they seek. In other words, they are co-constructing solutions as they speak. You don't have to problem solve first in order to find a solution. *The solution lies in looking at the situation with new eyes.* To quote Marcel Proust: "The real voyage of discovery consists not in seeking new landscapes, but in having new eyes."

Creating Affirmative Topics

Selecting the inquiry topic is partly an exercise in reframing. If you review the twenty-one workshop topics, each one has a positive edge to it. We can choose to focus on the deficiencies, the inadequacies, and the failures and go into problem-solving mode around issues, or we can explore the same issues in a way that imagines what it would be like when these issues are turned on their head and participants can co-create the best outcome. Affirmative topics are more than looking at the glass as half-full. The topic defines the scope of the inquiry because it sets the tone and substance of what will follow. Good topics are

- Stated in the affirmative

- Compelling or provocative and short

- Desirable—a situation you want to bring about

- Energizing, motivational, and within the realm of possibility

- Strategically important and of value to the organization and its members

In defining your own topics, it could be that you and other organizational members may already know what issues you need to inquire into, especially if they have come out of earlier workshops. If not, the interview protocol below will help you gain clarity around the inquiry topic relevant to your needs.

Using the four foundational questions bulleted below, organizational members are interviewed about high-point experiences in their work. The power that comes from organizational members talking about—and expanding on—their high-point experiences uncovers the life-giving forces of when they are operating at their best and helps define the affirmative topic. Through such interviews, you elicit is what it takes to operate optimally and that's what you want to amplify.

- What has been a high-point experience in your organization/division when you felt most alive, successful, and effective?

- Without being humble, what do you value most about yourself, your work, and your organization?

- What are the core factors that make this organization function at its best, when it feels a great place to be in, and without which it would cease to exist?

- Imagine it is three years into the future and the organization is just as you would want it to be. What's happening that makes it vibrant and successful? What has changed? What has stayed the same, and how have you contributed to this future?

(Adapted from Cooperrider, Whitney, & Stavros, 2008, p. 36).

The Interview Protocol

You will know from the twenty-one workshops in Part III, there is a template or format for the appreciative interview protocol. The interview protocol consists of two parts:

- "Lead-in" statement
- Interview questions

Lead-In Statement

The lead-in statement sets the scene and the tone and prepares the interviewees to focus on their personal experiences and stories that are life-nurturing regarding the topic of inquiry. The lead-in statement serves to ease people into the topic and, at the same time, must be compelling and inspirational, so that it helps people reach into their memories and best experiences of the past and also think of possibilities for the future—at a deeper and higher level than normal. Lead-ins create a picture of how, when things are working really fine, there is a very different reality. Lead-in statements are like bridges. They successfully describe the relationship between the topic and the personal or organizational vitality that the topic will deliver. Great lead-ins connect the whole person to the issue—rationally and emotionally—so that they can respond from a place of wholeness.

There are twenty-one examples of lead-in statements and questions in this book. The two examples below demonstrate shorter, simpler versions.

Affirmative Topic: THRIVING ON TRUST

Lead-in Statement: You can feel, hear, and see an open, trustworthy environment when you enter it. People are friendly, interested, busy, upbeat, smiling, and open with each other. They will tell you that they are listened to; their ideas count; they have policies, processes, and systems that help them do good work. They give and receive timely feedback, they encourage each other to be creative, be different, they demonstrate their own leadership at all times, and they can depend on each other.

- Remember a time when you experienced profound reciprocated trust with others. Please share your full story.

- How did having that trust affect your behavior, thoughts, and feelings?

Affirmative Topic: STRENGTH-BASED ORGANIZATIONAL DESIGNS

Lead-in Statement: The very best organizational designs ensure they are financially, socially, technically, and environmentally healthy. People know who's who, what's what, and where and why they are headed. They are clear about their organization's and its members' strengths, aligning the two through polices, processes, reward systems, and creating a culture of engagement and meaning. Most wonderfully, they connect the human spirit with organizational elements and technical systems.

- Remember a time when you were so engaged at work that time passed without your awareness; the activity you were involved in was meaningful to you and you couldn't help but do your best. Thinking back on that story, what existing organizational design elements helped you perform at your best to optimize your and the organization's performance?

- What additional elements would you introduce into your organization to build and strength its capacity and would wholeheartedly support and be proud of?

Interview Questions

The following summarizes the Appreciative Inquiry perspective on questions:

- Appreciative Inquiry emphasizes the art of crafting positive questions.

- We live in a world our questions create.

- Our questions determine the results we achieve.

- The more positive our question, the more it will create the possible.

- Our questions create movement and change.

If change begins with the very first questions we ask, questions are fateful in that they serve to guide the direction of any inquiry and the stories that are subsequently told. Ultimately, they determine the change direction for the organization. Appreciative Inquiry is the art of asking unconditionally positive questions to strengthen the system's capacity to anticipate and heighten positive potential.

Affirming interview questions are designed to reconnect the interviewees with their best past stories, successes, strengths, feelings of empowerment, positive characteristic and attributes, and so on. In reminding people of the best of the past and present, it becomes clearer that they can take the best into the future. We know from Appreciative Inquiry theory and principles, positive psychology, and other strength-based studies that in accessing memories of past best experiences arouses positive energy and enthusiasm, igniting imaginations that lead to positive action (Cooperrider, 1990).

Appreciative Inquiry questions can be viewed as being quite personal, so you may need to remind people that they have full control over what they disclose. When establishing the learning environment with the participants, it helps if you remind them that the learning environment needs to be respected as a safe place for individuals so that they can express themselves and share their ideas. The "realness" of the process and its inherent value are the foundations for learners co-creating their imagined, most desired future. Their voices are taken into account and they become participants, not just in the training room or the workshop, but in designing their own work in the future—they become co-designers of their own destiny, which is an empowering way of ensuring that any project they commit to will flourish, given leadership's support.

The distinguishing feature of the Appreciative Inquiry interview protocol is generativity: the creation and magnification of the best qualities that we discover about ourselves, each other, and our organizations. We achieve this through the conscious choice of uplifting and positively framed language in the affirmative topics and question protocols, both of which facilitate participants sharing stories in conversations with others. Outcomes of generative conversations include elevating and extending relationships through discovery; the invitation to imagine what else is possible; and the conscious co-design of meaningful realities with new, relevant, and dynamic rules of engagement. What you learn with and from each other becomes your blueprint for how you will begin to operate and continue to plan, learn, and adapt. The notion of *generative* in the Appreciative Inquiry context is explained by Gervase Bushe: "AI is generative in a number of ways. It is the quest for new ideas, images, theories, and models that liberate our collective aspirations, alter the social construction of reality and, in the process, make available decisions and actions that weren't available or didn't occur to us before. When successful, AI generates spontaneous, unsupervised, individual, group and organizational action toward a better future" (2007, p. 1).

Participants and Leadership

Who you choose to invite to attend a workshop will depend on your context and the objective. In organizations, the participant groups can be an intact team or department or a representative group of a number of teams or departments—either a vertical or a horizontal slice of the organization, with or without external stakeholders. Leaders are invited to participate equally as one of the many essential voices in the room. Given the opportunity to listen and hear the creative ideas, hopes, and dreams of their colleagues and organization stakeholders, leaders often recognize that their greatest contribution could be to get out of the way and let the members get on with it. Once positive energy is released, what supports it most are affirmation and a clear pathway for experimentation and innovation. As a participatory process, changes once begun continue in remarkable ways, with remarkable results. The best you can wish for from the organization's leadership is its sponsorship and, therefore, its willingness to embrace its responsibility as a positive change catalyst. Leaders, through their active support, facilitate the transformative process, as all organizational members step up to shape and live their shared destiny.

Valuing the Appreciative Inquiry Experience

Having invested in yourself through reading this book to help you design and deliver innovative, strength-based workshops framed in the Appreciative Inquiry worldview, what excites you about this work?

- What about the AI process most enlivens you and resonates with you?
- What excites you most about introducing AI into your work or personal life?
- What AI competencies or strengths have you discovered that you already have?
- What further imaginings do you have for yourself, your family, and your organization?
- What three wishes do you have for your future works with Appreciative Inquiry?
- What is one simple appreciative action that you can take immediately?

Closing Reflections

My goal in writing this book has been to share tools that help us all live from a place of greater consciousness: to be fully awake to the choices that will serve us whatever the situation. Some choices can set us off on an upward spiral, fueling us with greater excitement and energy, increasing our levels of satisfaction and joy, and enriching our experiences. Other choices can send us off on a downward spiral associated with energy loss, dissatisfaction, and feelings of life being sapped. If we can deliberately and consciously work toward increasing the upward spiral in our lives, then we are helping ourselves and others live with greater intentionality in finding what personally enriches us and those around us.

The form and process of Appreciative Inquiry with its underlying principles facilitates such upward spirals. A sweet blend of affirmative questions and positive language, delivered and received with open, curious minds and supportive dispositions, helps us wake up and open our eyes in appreciation of our gifts, our talents, and our aspirations. Most importantly, Appreciative Inquiry—with its positive and strength-based focus—is a heartfelt experience. The majority of leadership and change models emphasize the cognitive dimensions of change and development. A cognitive shift is important, but a heartfelt shift is transformative. Our whole being is impacted when a shift is heartfelt. One workshop can be transformative. One single positive experience, when we discover a latent talent or potential strength or experience a gesture of caring, can be transformative. In fact, the very first question asked, and the way it is asked, begins the change process. When we open ourselves to our best selves, envision possibilities, and get in touch with our strengths, a paradigmatic, seismic, quantum shift can happen in the blink of an eye. In homeopathic remedies, one mini drop can transform the entire body. In chaos theory, the beating of a butterfly's wings over China can cause weather turbulence over New York a month later. Similarly, the way a single question is framed can shift our very being. Very small changes in a system can alter its state forever.

Selected Bibliography

Barrett, F. (1998). Creativity and improvisation in jazz and organizations: Implications for organizational learning. *Organization Science, 9*(5), 605–622.

Barrett, F., & Fry, R.E. (2005). *Appreciative inquiry: A positive approach to building cooperative capacity.* Chagrin Falls, OH: Taos Institute.

Bascobert, K.J. (2005). *Appreciative living.* Wake Forest, NC: Venet Publishers.

Beecher, H.K. (1955, December 24). The powerful placebo. *Journal of the American Medical Association, 159*(17).

Brunner, R., & Emery, S. (2009). *Do you matter? How great design will make people love your company.* Upper Saddle River, NJ: FT Press.

Buckingham, M. (2007). *Go put your strengths to work.* New York: Simon and Schuster.

Buckingham, M., & Clifton, D.O. (2001). *Now, discover your strengths.* New York: Simon and Schuster.

Bushe, G.R. (2007). Appreciative inquiry is not (just) about the positive. *OD Practitioner, 39*(4), 30–35.

Cameron, K.S., Bright, D. Caza, A. (2004). Exploring the relationships between organizational virtuousness and performance. *American Behavioral Scientist,* 47: 766–790

Cameron, K.S., Dutton, J.E., & Quinn, R.E. (2003). *Positive organizational scholarship: Foundations of a new discipline.* San Francisco: Berrett-Koehler.

Cooperrider, D.L. (1990). Positive image, positive action: The affirmative basis of organizing. In S. Srivastva & D.L. Cooperrider (Eds.), *Appreciative management and leadership* (pp. 91–125). San Francisco, CA: Jossey-Bass.

Cooperrider, D.L. (n.d.). Positive image, positive action: The affirmative basis of organizing. Paper distributed in Appreciative Inquiry Certificate Program, Case Western Reserve University, Cleveland, Ohio.

Cooperrider, D.L., & Avital, M. (Eds.). (2004). *Advances in appreciative inquiry: Constructive discourse and human organization* (Vol. 1). Amsterdam: Elsevier.

Cooperrider, D.L., Whitney, D., & Stavros, J.M. (2003). *Appreciative inquiry handbook.* (1st ed.). Bedford Heights, OH: Lakeshore Publishers.

Cooperrider, D.L., Whitney, D., & Stavros, J.M. (2008). *Appreciative inquiry handbook.* (2nd ed.). Brunswick, OH: Crown Custom Publishing.

Csikszentmihalyi, M. (1990). *Flow: The psychology of optimal experience.* New York: Harper & Row.

Drucker, P. (1966). *The effective executive.* New York: HarperCollins.

Emery, M. (1989). *Participative design for participative democracy.* Canberra, ACT: Australian National University.

Emery, M., & Purser, R. (1996). *The search conference.* San Francisco: Jossey-Bass.

Findlay, J. (2003). Knowledge creation tools. Unpublished paper.

Fox, J. (2008). *Your child's strengths.* New York: Penguin.

Fredrickson, B.L. (2001). The role of positive emotions in positive psychology: The broaden-and-build theory of positive emotions. *American Psychologist, 56*(3), 218–226.

Fredrickson, B.L. (2003). Positive emotions and upward spirals in organizations (Chapter 11). In K. Cameron, J. Dutton, & R. Quinn (Eds.), *Positive organizational scholarship.* San Francisco: Berrett-Koehler.

Fredrickson, B.L. (2009). *Positivity.* New York: Crown.

Fredrickson, B.L., & Branigan, C. (2005). Positive emotions broaden the scope of attention and though-action repertoires. *Cognition and Emotion, 19*(3), 313–332.

Fredrickson, B.L., & Losada, M.F. (2005). Positive affect and the complex dynamics of human flourishing. *American Psychologist, 60*(7), 678–686.

Fredrickson, B.L., & Waugh, C.E. (2006). Nice to know you: Positive emotions, self–other overlap, and complex understanding in the formation of a new relationship. *The Journal of Positive Psychology, 1*(2), 93–106.

Fry, R.E., Barrett, F.J., Seiling, J., & Whitney, D. (2001). *Appreciative inquiry and organizational transformation: Reports from the field.* Westport, CT: Quorum Books.

Holzman, L. (2009). *Vygotsky at work and play.* New York: Psychology Press.

Kelly, T. (2001). *The art of innovation.* New York: Doubleday.

Kuhn, T.S. (1962). *The structure of scientific revolutions.* Chicago: University of Chicago Press.

Ludema, J.D., Whitney, D., Mohr, B.J., & Griffin, T.J. (2003). *The appreciative inquiry summit: A practitioner's guide for leading large group change.* San Francisco: Berrett-Koehler.

Owen H. (1997). *Open space technology: A user's guide.* San Francisco: Berrett-Koehler.

Owen H. (1999). *The spirit of leadership.* San Francisco: Berrett-Koehler.

Owen H. (2000). *The power of spirit.* San Francisco: Berrett-Koehler.

Owen, H. (2004). *The practice of peace.* Circle Pines MN: Human Systems Dynamics Institute.

Owen, H. (2008). *Wave rider: Leadership for high performance in a self-organizing world.* San Francisco: Berrett-Koehler.

Seligman, M. (1990). *Learned optimism: How to change your mind and your life.* New York: Simon and Schuster.

Seligman, M. (2002). *Authentic happiness: Using the new positive psychology to realize your potential for lasting fulfillment.* New York: The Free Press.

Seligman, M., & Csikszentmihalyi, M. (2000). Positive psychology: An introduction. *American Psychologist, 55*(1), 5–14.

Stavros, J., & Torres, C. (2005). *Dynamic relationships: Unleashing the power of appreciative inquiry in daily living.* Chagrin Falls, OH: Taos Institute.

Watkins, J.M., & Mohr, B.J. (2001). *Appreciative inquiry: Change at the speed of imagination.* San Francisco: Pfeiffer.

Wheatley, M.J. (2002). *Turning to one another.* San Francisco: Berrett-Koehler.

Whitney, D., Cooperrider, D., Trosten-Bloom, A., & Kaplin, B.S. (2002). *Encyclopedia of positive questions, Vol. 1.* Euclid, OH: Lakeshore Communications.

Whitney, D., & Trosten-Bloom, A. (2003). *The power of appreciative inquiry: A practical guide to positive change.* San Francisco: Berrett-Koehler.

Websites

AI Commons:
http://appreciativeinquiry.cwru.edu/

AI Listserv:
www.ailist@lists.business.utah.edu

Corporation for Positive Change:
www.positivechange.org/

Positive Matrix:
http://positivematrix.com.

Taos Institute:
www.taosinstitute.net.

TED TALKS Martin Seligman: *What positive psychology can help you become*
www.ted.com/index.php/talks/martin_seligman_on_the_state_of_
psychology.html

TED TALKS Mihaly Csikszentmihalyi: *Creativity, fulfillment and flow*
www.ted.com/index.php/talks/mihaly_csikszentmihalyi_on_flow.html

TED TALKS Ray Anderson on the *Business Logic of Sustainability*
www.ted.com/talks/lang/eng/ray_anderson_on_the_business_logic_
of_sustainability.html

About the Author

Robyn Stratton-Berkessel has been in the business of maximizing potential in a variety of capacities for over twenty years: teaching communications at university, developing and leading sales teams, managing a training and development consultancy practice serving global clients, and establishing her own firm in 1992. Robyn has presented at thought-leadership conferences internationally on the subject of change and strength-based approaches to innovation and leadership. She collaboratively designs ways to energize people and their enterprise by uncovering their existing strengths and discovering the system's positive core. Outcomes are extraordinary personal breakthroughs, unleashing the best in individuals—resulting in an energized enterprise with more mindful, engaged employee performance and caring relationships. Robyn works in partnership with senior executives, managers, and teams across functional, political, cultural, and geographic boundaries in professional services firms, health and consumer goods organizations, financial services, and telecommunications. She has been a catalyst to bring about measurable, meaningful, and transformative results. A graduate of the University of Sydney and with a master's of organizational systems from Monash University, Melbourne, Australia, Robyn is committed to continuous learning and development and sharing it. Robyn's firm is L.I.T. Consulting Incorporated; her website and blog can be found at http://positivematrix.com. Robyn would be very happy to hear from you at robyn@positivematrix.com

Pfeiffer Publications Guide

This guide is designed to familiarize you with the various types of Pfeiffer publications. The formats section describes the various types of products that we publish; the methodologies section describes the many different ways that content might be provided within a product. We also provide a list of the topic areas in which we publish.

FORMATS

In addition to its extensive book-publishing program, Pfeiffer offers content in an array of formats, from fieldbooks for the practitioner to complete, ready-to-use training packages that support group learning.

FIELDBOOK Designed to provide information and guidance to practitioners in the midst of action. Most fieldbooks are companions to another, sometimes earlier, work, from which its ideas are derived; the fieldbook makes practical what was theoretical in the original text. Fieldbooks can certainly be read from cover to cover. More likely, though, you'll find yourself bouncing around following a particular theme, or dipping in as the mood, and the situation, dictate.

HANDBOOK A contributed volume of work on a single topic, comprising an eclectic mix of ideas, case studies, and best practices sourced by practitioners and experts in the field.

An editor or team of editors usually is appointed to seek out contributors and to evaluate content for relevance to the topic. Think of a handbook not as a ready-to-eat meal, but as a cookbook of ingredients that enables you to create the most fitting experience for the occasion.

RESOURCE Materials designed to support group learning. They come in many forms: a complete, ready-to-use exercise (such as a game); a comprehensive resource on one topic (such as conflict management) containing a variety of methods and approaches; or a collection of like-minded activities (such as icebreakers) on multiple subjects and situations.

TRAINING PACKAGE An entire, ready-to-use learning program that focuses on a particular topic or skill. All packages comprise a guide for the facilitator/trainer and a workbook for the participants. Some packages are supported with additional media—such as video—or learning aids, instruments, or other devices to help participants understand concepts or practice and develop skills.

- *Facilitator/trainer's guide* Contains an introduction to the program, advice on how to organize and facilitate the learning event, and step-by-step instructor notes. The guide also contains copies of presentation materials—handouts, presentations, and overhead designs, for example—used in the program.

- *Participant's workbook* Contains exercises and reading materials that support the learning goal and serves as a valuable reference and support guide for participants in the weeks and months that follow the learning event. Typically, each participant will require his or her own workbook.

ELECTRONIC CD-ROMs and web-based products transform static Pfeiffer content into dynamic, interactive experiences. Designed to take advantage of the searchability, automation, and ease-of-use that technology provides, our e-products bring convenience and immediate accessibility to your workspace.

METHODOLOGIES

CASE STUDY A presentation, in narrative form, of an actual event that has occurred inside an organization. Case studies are not prescriptive, nor are they used to prove a point; they are designed to develop critical analysis and decision-making skills. A case study has a specific time frame, specifies a sequence of events, is narrative in structure, and contains a plot structure—an issue (what should be/have been done?). Use case studies when the goal is to enable participants to apply previously learned theories to the circumstances in the case, decide what is pertinent, identify the real issues, decide what should have been done, and develop a plan of action.

ENERGIZER A short activity that develops readiness for the next session or learning event. Energizers are most commonly used after a break or lunch to stimulate or refocus the group. Many involve some form of physical activity, so they are a useful way to counter post-lunch lethargy. Other uses include transitioning from one topic to another, where "mental" distancing is important.

EXPERIENTIAL LEARNING ACTIVITY (ELA) A facilitator-led intervention that moves participants through the learning cycle from experience to application (also known as a Structured Experience). ELAs are carefully thought-out designs in which there is a definite learning purpose and intended outcome. Each step—everything that participants do during the activity—facilitates the accomplishment of the stated goal. Each ELA includes complete instructions for facilitating the intervention and a clear statement of goals, suggested group size and timing, materials required, an explanation of the process, and, where appropriate, possible variations to the activity. (For more detail on Experiential Learning Activities, see the Introduction to the *Reference Guide to Handbooks and Annuals*, 1999 edition, Pfeiffer, San Francisco.)

GAME A group activity that has the purpose of fostering team spirit and togetherness in addition to the achievement of a pre-stated goal. Usually contrived—undertaking a desert expedition, for example—this type of learning method offers an engaging means for participants to demonstrate and practice business and interpersonal skills. Games are effective for team building and personal development mainly because the goal is subordinate to the process—the means through which participants reach decisions, collaborate, communicate, and generate trust and understanding. Games often engage teams in "friendly" competition.

ICEBREAKER A (usually) short activity designed to help participants overcome initial anxiety in a training session and/or to acquaint the participants with one another. An icebreaker can be a fun activity or can be tied to specific topics or training goals. While a useful tool in itself, the icebreaker comes into its own in situations where tension or resistance exists within a group.

INSTRUMENT A device used to assess, appraise, evaluate, describe, classify, and summarize various aspects of human behavior. The term used to describe an instrument depends primarily on its format and purpose. These terms include survey, questionnaire, inventory, diagnostic, survey, and poll. Some uses of instruments include providing instrumental feedback to group members, studying here-and-now processes or functioning within a group, manipulating group composition, and evaluating outcomes of training and other interventions.

Instruments are popular in the training and HR field because, in general, more growth can occur if an individual is provided with a method for focusing specifically on his or her own behavior. Instruments also are used to obtain information that will serve as a basis for change and to assist in workforce planning efforts.

Paper-and-pencil tests still dominate the instrument landscape with a typical package comprising a facilitator's guide, which offers advice on administering the instrument and interpreting the collected data, and an initial set of instruments. Additional instruments are available separately. Pfeiffer, though, is investing heavily in e-instruments. Electronic instrumentation provides effortless distribution and, for larger groups particularly, offers advantages over paper-and-pencil tests in the time it takes to analyze data and provide feedback.

LECTURETTE A short talk that provides an explanation of a principle, model, or process that is pertinent to the participants' current learning needs. A lecturette is intended to establish a common language bond between the trainer and the participants by providing a mutual frame of reference. Use a lecturette as an introduction to a group activity or event, as an interjection during an event, or as a handout.

MODEL A graphic depiction of a system or process and the relationship among its elements. Models provide a frame of reference and something more tangible, and more easily remembered, than a verbal explanation. They also give participants something to "go on," enabling them to track their own progress as they experience the dynamics, processes, and relationships being depicted in the model.

ROLE PLAY A technique in which people assume a role in a situation/scenario: a customer service rep in an angry-customer exchange, for example. The way in which the role is approached is then discussed and feedback is offered. The role play is often repeated using a different approach and/or incorporating changes made based on feedback received. In other words, role playing is a spontaneous interaction involving realistic behavior under artificial (and safe) conditions.

SIMULATION A methodology for understanding the interrelationships among components of a system or process. Simulations differ from games in that they test or use a model that depicts or mirrors some aspect of reality in form, if not necessarily in content. Learning occurs by studying the effects of change on one or more factors of the model. Simulations are commonly used to test hypotheses about what happens in a system—often referred to as "what if?" analysis—or to examine best-case/worst-case scenarios.

THEORY A presentation of an idea from a conjectural perspective. Theories are useful because they encourage us to examine behavior and phenomena through a different lens.

TOPICS

The twin goals of providing effective and practical solutions for workforce training and organization development and meeting the educational needs of training and human resource professionals shape Pfeiffer's publishing program. Core topics include the following:

Leadership & Management

Communication & Presentation

Coaching & Mentoring

Training & Development

E-Learning

Teams & Collaboration

OD & Strategic Planning

Human Resources

Consulting

What will you find on pfeiffer.com?

- The best in workplace performance solutions for training and HR professionals
- Downloadable training tools, exercises, and content
- Web-exclusive offers
- Training tips, articles, and news
- Seamless on-line ordering
- Author guidelines, information on becoming a Pfeiffer Partner, and much more

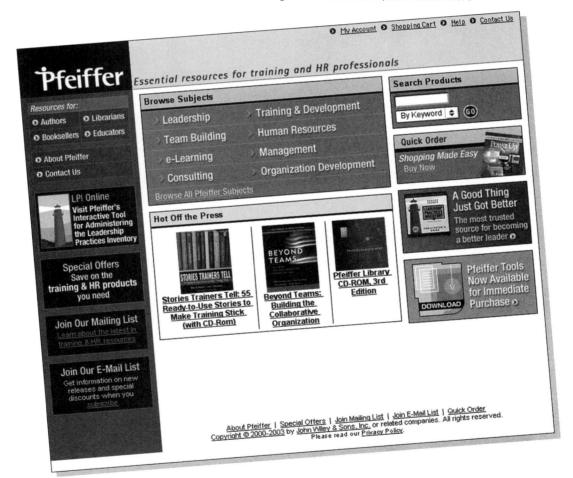

Discover more at www.pfeiffer.com